QUEEN ELIZABETH HOUSE
INTERNATIONAL DEVELOPMENT CENTRE

INDIA'S EMERGENCE AS AN INDUSTRIAL POWER

The Royal Institute of International Affairs is an unofficial body which promotes the scientific study of international questions and does not express opinions of its own. The opinions expressed in this publication are the responsibility of the author.

The Institute and its Research Committee are grateful for the comments and suggestions made by Dr V.N. Balasubramanyan and Professor Michael Lipton, who were asked to review the manuscript of this book.

Richard Thomas is a member of the British Diplomatic Service. This book, written during a sabbatical year at the Royal Institute of International Affairs, is a purely personal view of a current issue and is not based in any way on material not available for public use.

India's Emergence as an Industrial Power

Middle Eastern Contracts

RICHARD THOMAS

C. HURST & COMPANY, LONDON
and ARCHON BOOKS, HAMDEN,
CONNECTICUT 06514
for the Royal Institute of International Affairs, London
1982

First published in the United Kingdom by
C. Hurst and Co. (Publishers) Ltd.,
38 King Street, Covent Garden, London WC2E 8JT
and Archon Books, an imprint of
The Shoe String Press, Inc.,
995 Sherman Avenue,
Hamden, Connecticut 06514

ISBNs
Hurst: 0-905838-56-4
Archon: 0-208-01974-X

© Royal Institute of International Affairs 1982

Printed by
LIBRA PRESS LTD.
56 Wong Chuk Hang Road 5D, Hong Kong

CONTENTS

FOREWORD

THE image of India as exporter of industrial products and technology will probably be new to all but the specialist observer of the industrial and contracting scene at the international level. The recent development of Indian industry and technology, now measured by the ability to win major foreign contracts in competition with the advanced industrial countries, has passed largely unnoticed. Using evidence mainly from the Middle East, this book investigates India's emergence as a competitor to the established exporters and considers some of the circumstances that accompany it both at home and abroad.

The challenge of the newly industrializing countries has been a recurring theme in European and American discussions of industrial adjustment and economic recovery since the mid-1970s. Again, the popular image of a NIC is more often of such Asian countries as Taiwan, the Republic of Korea, Hong Kong, and Singapore than of such large and diverse economies as those of Brazil and India—except perhaps in the textiles sector. A parallel study, *The NICs: Trade and Adjustment Implications*, edited by Louis Turner of Chatham House and Neil McMullen of the National Planning Association, Washington, DC, analyses the nature of the challenge posed by the major NICs in a number of industrial sectors, including those in which India is strong. The present volume focuses specifically on India, as a country which displays some of the qualities of a newly industrializing country, some symptoms of industrial stagnation, and some of the classic characteristics of underdevelopment—with a political élite whose attitude remains ambivalent towards the process of industrialization.

The main work on the book was undertaken during the Janata administration of Morarji Desai. Just as the author was reaching the end of his secondment to Chatham House, the Janata government fell and Mr Desai retired from public life. Mrs Gandhi's election victory in January 1980, representing a major political upheaval, was bound to affect the balance of interests in Indian industry and the relationship between government and the industrial sector; already within her first twelve months in power there have been a number of controversial decisions about the allocation of contracts and the direction of investment. It remains, however, a relatively safe prediction that official encouragement in India will continue to be given to engineering exports. The issues raised in this volume thus retain their central relevance to Mrs Gandhi's second government— and, perhaps, to its successors. They will be relevant, also, to the established exporters, who face competition on the international market from a new source.

Chatham House   WILLIAM WALLACE
                                                   Director of Studies

ACKNOWLEDGEMENTS

I am profoundly grateful to my enlightened employer, the Foreign and Commonwealth Office, for having allowed me the time to make this study, and to the Royal Institute of International Affairs, for having welcomed me into Chatham House as a research fellow. At Chatham House, under the kindly tutelage of the Director, Mr David Watt, and the Director of Studies, Dr William Wallace, I was fortunate to be able to draw on the corporate wisdom and support of the research and library staffs. There too I experienced that mixture of alarming stimulus and helpful interest, the study group, one of which was arranged round my project. My thanks are due to all its members for giving so freely of their time and energy in discussion and constructive criticism, but perhaps especially to Sir Terence Garvey, who chaired the group with the incisive élan that he brought to bear on the conduct of Indo-British relations during his time as British High Commissioner in New Delhi; to Mr Kenneth Warner of Grindlays Bank, who not only contributed valuable papers but also arranged for me to receive expert guidance from his colleagues in Bombay; and to Miss Patsy Harvey of the Foreign and Commonwealth Office, who both suggested the theme and acted as a general morale booster whenever, as happened more than once, I thought I had come up against a dead-end in my inquiries. I am also indebted to Miss Harvey's colleagues in the FCO, especially Mr Tom Butlin, for their help with some of the statistics, as indeed I am to the London office of the Engineering Export Promotion Council of India.

I pestered a good many of my colleagues in British diplomatic posts throughout Asia, Africa, and the Middle East, and through some of them I also made great demands on Indian diplomats working in Iraq, Kuwait, Libya, Saudi Arabia, and the United Arab Emirates. All these people replied to my letters with care and understanding, a courtesy that for many has gone unacknowledged till now, and the Indian embassies concerned were kind enough to draw up the lists of contracts and joint ventures which form the bases of Appendices 20 to 24. I am also greatly indebted to the many Indian officials and businessmen who supplied me with much of the data on which this study is based, and to some in particular, such as Mr W. S. Tambe of the Reserve Bank of India and the BHEL project management staff at Jizan in Saudi Arabia, whose kind hospitality I so much enjoyed. I was also the fortunate recipient of generous hospitality and help from other kind friends, for example Mr and Mrs Charat Ram of New Delhi and Mr and Mrs Colin Fox of Dubai, whose only connection with my research was that they happened to live in places that I wished to visit, and from long-suffering Diplomatic Service and locally employed colleagues in all my ports of call.

I picked the brains of academics working in the same field; without exception they readily shared their knowledge with me. Mr Sanjaya Lall of the Institute of Economics and Statistics, University of Oxford, was particularly generous in this respect. At a later stage I profited from the helpful comments of the two Readers of the work.

Finally, I should like to thank Miss Elizabeth Watson of Chatham House for typing and retyping the various drafts and Miss Rena Fenteman, the Chatham House research staff editor, for all her skill, advice, and hard work in preparing this study for publication.

Prague   R.T.
December 1980

INTRODUCTION

Not far from the Red Sea port of Jizan in the extreme south of Saudi Arabia there is a large construction encampment consisting, like so many others in that rapidly changing and developing country, of neat rows of prefabricated aluminium portable buildings, studded with the rear ends of countless air conditioners and surmounted by an unlovely array of water tanks and television aerials. Parked along the whitewashed kerbstones is a number of Japanese cars. In front of the larger buildings are makeshift gardens in which kerosene tins doing retirement duty under a fresh coat of paint contain a crop of canna lilies and mother-in-law's tongue. The camp has a look of efficient comfort in adverse conditions, suggesting that its occupants are adaptable and capable people who are not unaccustomed to working in harsh surroundings but who value the softer and homelier appurtenances of living and must make do for the time being with surrogates.

The camp houses Indians. It is in fact the headquarters of an Indian project which sprawls over an area of 900 square kilometres. In the camp live some 1,100 skilled and unskilled men—engineers, linesmen, mechanics, masons, carpenters, fitters, riggers, and plain labourers—brought together in this distant corner of Saudi Arabia in order to supply the modern benefits of electricity. They come from all parts of India and speak between them probably a dozen languages, but the language of the project is English, the only one they nearly all have in common.

This is a turnkey project. It consists of the construction of a 42 MW diesel power station and a housing complex for the people who will run it, together with the installation of all the necessary transmission and distribution equipment—270 km of line and 175 substations—to bring electricity to 8,000 new consumers dotted about the sparsely populated countryside of the Wadi Jizan. (A turnkey project is one that involves the design, procurement, erection, and commissioning of all the equipment, and the completion of all the civil works, so that the project is ready for operation.)

The Indian company that won this contract is Bharat Heavy Electricals Ltd (BHEL). As its name implies, BHEL is not concerned solely with erection and installation. It is mainly a manufacturer, and much of the equipment being put together at Jizan is Indian-made, by BHEL. Working alongside BHEL are two subcontractors, again Indian: Engineering Projects (India) Ltd, responsible for civil works, and Bombay Suburban Electric Supply Ltd, which is doing the transmission and distribution work. The consultants are Taiwanese and British. The project is on schedule, and BHEL expects to make a reasonable profit from it.

I have chosen to introduce the book in this way because what is going on at Jizan exemplifies in the compass of a single project what the book is about. Take the popular misconceptions first. India is surely poor—terrifyingly so—and under-developed, a consumer of foreign aid, a recipient of other people's technologies. India is an agricultural country, with a colossal population of subsistence peasants. Indian industry, what there is of it, is concerned with India's own needs, not those of countries like Saudi Arabia, rich beyond the dreams of avarice. And yet here at Jizan, and at a number of other places in the Middle East, are Indians putting together the products of Indian industry in a foreign country.

Even at a considerably shallower depth of misconception one still encounters surprise, even if not downright disbelief, if one suggests that Indian electrical engineering exports could perhaps be on the verge of making a sizeable dent in world markets. How could India, notorious for its appalling power shortages, possibly have capacity to spare for exports of heavy electrical equipment? Surely BHEL, a public-sector corporation, should be under orders from the government of India to put India's own energy house in order before venturing into the Saudi Arabian desert? And in any case, these more knowledgeable sceptics point out, the Indian public sector is woefully inefficient and *a priori* unfitted for tasks beyond the frontiers of India.

I hope the book will help to clear up some of these misconceptions. It is time that some of the achievements of the 'new' India of modern industry and technology were more widely known, and this book, which focuses on India's industrial exports to other developing countries, mainly in the Middle East, may go a little way towards that end. For, in these exports, one can perceive within a comprehensible compass the variety and extent of Indian industrial capability. With no pretence to be an exhaustive economic analysis it is an attempt to gather up the facts (what sorts and quantities of capital goods Indian companies are exporting, what sorts and sizes of projects they are involved in, the contribution made by Indian migrant labour, and where the main markets are) and to deduce from them a little of what the future holds for India as an exporter of goods and technology. An India involved industrially in the

Middle East and elsewhere will inevitably have a rather different outlook on world affairs from that of the India of the recent past, engrossed solely in its own economic development. But I leave it to others to attempt the politico-strategic speculations which flow from this thought.

Inevitably some of the material describing these achievements may be considered dull. For most British and other Western readers, however, it will be largely new, and I therefore make no apology for setting it out at some length, particularly in chapters 2 and 3. But, recognizing that lists and catalogues make tedious prose, I have banished as many of them as I dare to the notes and appendices.

The book has two objectives: to document India's recent progress in industrial exporting, and then, in chapter 7, briefly to canvass the notion of Indian collaboration with Western firms in third countries. For historical reasons the Western example chosen is Britain, but what is true of Britain is in almost all cases just as true of, say, the United States or the Netherlands. India's emergence into the field of international contracting could be interpreted as a threat to British and other Western commercial interests. But it could also turn out to be a positive challenge to collaboration in third markets.

India has been involved with Western countries for upwards of 400 years. Until recently the involvement with Britain was so close as to be almost integral. One of the results of decolonization has been that the deliberate disengagement between India and Britain has grown wider than either of them expected when it was set in train, so much so that the notion of collaborating with Indians in a commercial enterprise in a third country strikes many British businessmen, as indeed it does most of their Western counterparts, as improbable. And yet it was not always so, and something might be gained from renewing old links, and forging new ones, in today's rather different circumstances. Indian and British firms should slot well together. Their executives and specialists speak the same language, literally, and, in a number of important ways, figuratively too. Indian suppliers are closer than their European or North American equivalents to many of today's more dynamic markets (particularly the Middle East), Indian labour is plentiful at all levels of skill and generally less demanding than the Western, including British, equivalent. Indian engineers and draughtsmen earn far less than their Western opposite numbers, so Indian engineering should be a pretty good bargain. These Indian strengths complement a number of British ones. British technology is more advanced, British firms are generally more experienced in overseas markets and are better known. Their managerial and marketing skills are likely (though not necessarily so) to be more advanced than those of equivalent Indian firms. These factors seem self-evident, and yet there are very few examples of Indo-British collaboration in joint ventures in third countries, fewer than there are, say, of Indo-Japanese or Indo-German collaboration of this sort.

Of course I realize that, at a time of high unemployment in the developed countries, especially Britain, any suggestion that smacks of exporting jobs to India is hardly likely to strike an instantly sympathetic chord. Why, the Western reader might well ask, should Western firms be encouraged to take on only half a project in, say, Saudi Arabia, leaving the other half to an Indian firm? Why not put in for the whole thing, with double the profit and employment opportunities, and none of the risks and complications inherent in a collaboration with a firm from a developing country? The answer is so simple that it hardly needs stating. But, at the risk of being accused of over-simplification and naivety, I shall state it nevertheless: half a contract is better than no contract, and half a jumbo contract may be considerably better than a whole run-of-the-mill contract. Projects tend to grow in size and complexity, as probably will the competitiveness of India and other LDCs.

I

From Import Substitution
to Exporting

INDIAN ministers and newspapers often claim that India is the
world's tenth (sometimes ninth or eighth) industrial power. Presumably they mean by this that India ranks tenth in the value of her
total industrial production, or perhaps of manufacturing alone. Even
though this is a misleading claim,[1] it does serve a purpose. It startles
the audience (it is meant to). India *is* industrialized, very heavily in
some ways, and some of her industry is very advanced. Many of its
products are exported, as is some of the technology that leads to
their production. The point that these ministers and newspapers are
trying to drive home (never mind the accuracy of their statistics) is
that India, not so long ago an almost exclusively agrarian country,
is now also an industrial one. She has achieved much of this transformation through the efforts of her own entrepreneurs and public
sector development, the latter assisted, but rarely dominated, by
foreign aid. The contribution of transnational corporations has been
far less marked than in, say, Brazil. Other developing countries could
well be advised to profit from her experience and expertise. This
applies both to those LDCs with factor endowments and problems
similar to India's, which could learn from India's achievements and
mistakes, and to those with very different circumstances which could
benefit from India's relatively higher development. A capital-rich
but skill-starved African country, for instance, could assist itself and
India by drawing on the latter's reserves of engineers.

Industry is very unevenly distributed over the country. There are
areas, particularly the Bihar/West Bengal coalfield and Bombay and
its hinterland, where the presence of industry is as all-pervading as
it is in the Ruhr or the southern part of Yorkshire. Many of India's
industries were established as more or less green-field exercises. They
did not grow organically out of earlier industries: as a result, and
probably inevitably, they were vertically integrated. Successive

governments have attempted to spread the effects, good and bad, of industrialization horizontally by encouraging the natural growth of small-scale feeder industries round the heavy centres. This policy has worked, to the extent that small-scale satellite industries, both downstream and upstream, now exist in abundance. Many of them are undoubtedly inefficient and stay in business only as a result of liberal and skilful use of the various government aids available for the small-scale sector. But it is also true that many others are genuine success stories, unencumbered by the bureaucratic deadweight that so bedevils much of India's public sector. They still congregate too closely round the centres of activity, and Mr Morarji Desai's Janata government seemed determined to spread the benefits far wider. It was indicated that, under the Sixth Five Year Plan, the emphasis would be shifted still further from 'large houses'[2] and heavy industry through the encouragement of cottage industry (already nicknamed the 'tiny sector'), with a ban on new industrial licensing in urban areas with a population of over 500,000.[3]

Any Indian government, whatever its political credo, is bound to do what it can to maintain the cohesiveness of Indian society and resist tendencies towards a widening split between the two Indias, between the new industrialized India and village India. But in a way the damage has already been done; planning and administrative measures to restrict the growth of existing industry amount to little more than attempts to shut the stable door after some of the horses have bolted, and possibly involve considerable risk to the health of those that remain. Whatever one's view of the desirability or otherwise of Indian industrial policy, the fact remains that there is a 'new India' existing alongside the traditional 'village' India. Of course this is a crude over-simplification, but there is more than a grain of truth in it and it can serve a useful illustrative purpose.

By 1977 India's population had reached about 650 million, and it is growing by about 2.5 per cent a year. Subsistence farmers and landless labourers account for the great bulk of the population. They speak fifteen 'scheduled' languages and another 1,637 officially recognized 'mother tongues'. They live in 576,000 villages. Only about one-third of them are literate. Their per capita income in 1976 was about £75,[4] making them collectively among the world's poorest people.

The 'new India' is to be found in the towns, of which there are 2,600 or so with an urban population of some 130 million,[5] roughly 10 per cent of whom are English-speaking. These 13 million or so people use English at work, and, more often than not, at home. They even think in it. They have to, since English is the only language they have in common with all their counterparts throughout the country. It is the medium of administration, defence, commerce, law, and higher education. Thirteen million may not seem very many (only 2 per cent) among 650 million, but their distribution is what matters. They are India's managers. They are present in, and generally in charge of, every sphere of activity with which foreign commercial enterprises are likely to come in contact. And, immediately below them in the hierarchies of most of these activities, and certainly so in manufacturing and construction, are tens of millions who understand and speak some English. They are the skilled and semi-skilled, the operatives in the factories and the draughtsmen in the engineering offices, and together they work in occupations, and even conditions, that have more in common with those obtaining in Birmingham or Lille than in traditional village India.

This is the developed side of India, a country with a wide spread of modern industries making everything from nuclear reactors to textile machinery, from machine tools to petrochemical plant. It is a far cry from traditional India, but nevertheless it is dependent on it, just as dependent as ever the princes and zemindars were, in an India that has in recent years (disasters excepted) proved to be capable of self-sufficiency in food. The modest surplus produced by the 80 per cent who live on the land feeds the 20 per cent who live in the towns. The margins are very narrow, and when, as in the middle Sixties and the early Seventies, the monsoon fails, India's economy suffers a major setback. Domestic demand wilts and foreign exchange reserves are spent on imports of foodgrains instead of industrial raw materials and components. Better storage facilities and higher stocks of grain will gradually reduce the impact of drought on foreign currency reserves, but there is little that can be done in the way of improvements to the infrastructure to lessen its impact on domestic demand. If the peasants have no surpluses to sell they are going to have very little to spend on the products of industrial India, at least until the next harvest. Increased attention to exporting in recent years probably owes more to low domestic demand, for whatever reason, than to any number of official blandishments.

India is as often as not nowadays classed with a mixed group of developing countries collectively known by those who think they have reason to fear them—the older developed countries—as the 'newly industrializing countries' or NICs.[6] It is not a particularly apt description of India, but it is one that India will probably have to live with, however misleading it may be, and however wrong an impression it might convey to the outsider. It is misleading for two main reasons. First, India's industrialization is by no means all new. Indeed many of India's industrial problems have a depressing and familiar British ring to them: old, outdated plant, particularly in textiles (some of it dating back into the nineteenth century); 'sick' industries in need of rescue by semi or full nationalization; sluggish investment. A far cry from the thrusting new electronics factories of Taiwan and Hong Kong, and admittedly (and fortunately for India) far from universally typical. And second, the term 'industrializing' has a dynamic connotation that is perhaps not altogether suited to a country governed, as it was, from 1977 to 1980, by a party intent on slowing the pace of industrialization as we understand the term in favour of rural craft industries and agriculture,[7] even if the object was only to correct the pro-industrial biases that have long characterized the Indian economy.

Industrialization has been going on in India for well over a hundred years. Throughout the greater part of the nineteenth century cotton and jute mills were being established and railways were being built. It is true that the Raj did little to encourage the growth of industry (India was far too valuable a captive market for exports of British manufactures),[8] but nevertheless it grew, much of it as the result of indigenous entrepreneurial effort, epitomized by the Tata family's steel mill at Jamshedpur, once the largest in the Commonwealth and still going strong.[9] The *swadeshi* or 'buy Indian' movement, founded in 1907 as a form of economic protest against British rule, helped local entrepreneurs to find a market for their goods, and the effect of the Second World War was both to shut off much of the British competition, which had either been switched into war production or prevented from reaching India by transport dislocation and blockade, or both, and to boost the output of those Indian industries which could be of use in the war effort.

But it was after Independence, and particularly during the early years of planning, that Indian industrialization really got under way, with the establishment in the public sector of massive basic industries such as iron and steel, fertilizers, coal, heavy engineering, and heavy electrical equipment.[10] Nehru believed in development through industrialization and his object was to make India industrially self-sufficient right across the board rather than to concentrate on a few industries selected for their growth or export potential, as has been the case in most of the other, more typical, NICs. India's industrial strategy during the Fifties had much in common with the Soviet Union's a generation earlier, and was partly modelled on it, with Soviet financial aid and technology heavily committed in the process.[11] Western governments were also involved in the building of the public sector; the Germans in steel, the Americans in heavy electricals, and the British in both. And, taking their cue from government directives favouring investment in the 'core' sector,[12] firms that would otherwise have been denied a share in India's increasingly protected market moved into the heavy end of Indian industry, particularly in fertilizers, petrochemicals, and electrical equipment, but also into engineering and vehicle building.

As the manufacturing sector grew in size and complexity so there arose a steadily greater need for consultancy services and thus greater opportunities for indigenous enterprises to provide them. India now has more than 150 large and medium-sized consultancy firms (i.e. employing from 15 to over 1,000 professional staff) in the public and the private sector. They cover the same wide range as Indian industry itself. Indian consultants are now exporting their experience of building capital goods and setting up plants in other developing (and developed) countries. They are men who have overseen the transformation in the space of a single generation of a lightly industrialized developing country into a major industrial power. Their experience is thus considerable, and it was gained on the job. Their skills should therefore be highly marketable, particularly in other developing countries, or to firms in high-cost developed countries looking for contracts in the Third World.[13]

India's industries have grown up behind high protective barriers. A rigid policy of import substitution meant, until very recently, that if a capital item or component was made in India, however inadequately, with however much delay, or even at times however theoretically, then that item was a prohibited import. (Imports of consumer goods were virtually banned.) Not only were Indian industrial concerns protected from the effects of outside competition, they were also to be provided with a considerable measure of protection from one another through the operation of the Monopolies and Restrictive Trade Practices Act (MRTPA),[14] one effect of which would have been to shield less efficient firms from the results of the growth that their more successful competitors would otherwise achieve. But the Janata government had a change of heart. The MRTPA had so far proved more of a threat than an instrument in actual use, and industry was being gradually exposed to more outside competition as a result of a policy of selective but fairly widespread import liberalization.[15] As the authors of the Draft Sixth Five Year Plan put it, 'the strategy of import substitution can now be made more flexible and reflect domestic resource cost considerations so that, on the margin, further growth of extremely inefficient import-substituting capacity may be slowed down.'[16]

Recognition that rigid import substitution breeds inefficiency may not be the whole reason for India's switch to a more outward-looking trade policy. It is true that, put another way, this amounted to an admission by the Indian government that it could not afford not to permit some measure of import liberalization. But it is at least questionable whether this apparent imperative would have carried quite so much conviction if there had been a balance of payments crisis either in being or threatening during the early months of 1978 which preceded the decision to liberalize. It is a reasonable assumption that the healthy state of the reserves (see Appendix 1 below) helped tip the balance of the argument. In other words, for the first time for some years India could afford to import more freely.

It might be reasonable to assume that, in deciding to liberalize imports in 1978, India's administrators were thinking at least partly in terms of giving exporting industries a shot in the arm, particularly as the government's annual *Economic Survey* had only shortly before confirmed the importance of having an import policy which promoted 'a continuing and large growth in exports', since a 'growing export sector has an important role to play in domestic development'.[17] In fact, however, the liberalization measures, which were non-discriminatory, were accompanied by a reduction in some of the incentives to exporters which had previously obtained. The government may have been counting on the relatively greater attraction of exporting resulting from the natural diminution of rewards from import substitution that theoretically follows import liberalization. Or it may simply have been unintentional. It surely cannot have escaped the government's notice that inward remittances alone could not be expected to maintain for ever the healthy balance of payments needed to sustain the import liberalization. Anyway the 1979 import policy in the event restored some of the export incentives, notably in the provisions for duty exemption and in allowing the import of project equipment used in project exports abroad.[18]

Indian exports, at about 7 per cent of GNP, are considerably more marginal to what is, after all, virtually a continental economy than they are to a trading nation like the UK or Japan. Comparatively minor fluctuations in economic activity at home can therefore have disproportionate effects on exports. For instance in some years India has exported steel, but regular markets have not been built up because in other years there has been none to export, either because a surge in domestic demand has outstripped supply or because supplies have dropped owing to input shortages or because of labour difficulties. There seems little doubt that the steep increase in engineering exports that started in the middle Seventies was due as much to slack domestic demand as to the result of any conscious efforts by the government to reduce the impact of the 1973/4 oil price increases by exporting more. Indeed one view expressed by a number of Indian businessmen and officials in the Gulf—perhaps a slightly jaundiced view—is that India, far from foreseeing the

Middle Eastern spending spree as she would have done had she helped to create it by promoting exports there, was in fact taken by surprise and was not immediately able to take full advantage of it.

Whatever one's view of the cause and effect, there can be no gainsaying the steep rise in Indian 'non-traditional' exports, especially engineering goods, worldwide but more particularly to Middle Eastern and North African OPEC countries. In 1966/7 engineering goods accounted for only 3.6 per cent of Indian exports. Ten years later this proportion had risen to 10.7 per cent. In 1966/7 18.9 per cent of those engineering goods went to the Middle Eastern OPEC countries and Libya (a more impressive sounding performance than it really was, since the 18.9 per cent represented a total of only Rs. 5.81 crore), but by 1976/7 this proportion had risen to 31.7 per cent (in cash terms, Rs. 174.72 crore). Appendices 4 and 5 below illustrate this major increase more fully. When in 1978/9 domestic demand at last started to pick up and the growth of engineering exports began to falter[19] the initial reaction in official circles was to assume that exports would be bound to suffer and that there was no alternative to a downward revision of the 1979/80 government target for engineering exports, from Rs. 850 crore to Rs. 820 crore. The reason given by the industry's representatives (principally the Engineering Export Promotion Council and the Association of Indian Engineering Industry) was that firms should use 1979/80 to 'strengthen the domestic production base by effecting modernization and enlarging their capacities for a sustained long-term growth in engineering exports.'[20] By March 1979, however, the target was back to Rs. 850 crore. The 1980/1 target had meanwhile remained at Rs. 1,000 crore. This episode perhaps demonstrated the government's realization that India had become too dependent on expectations of increased earnings from exports of engineering goods to be able to afford the luxury of treating them as an expendable margin. The targets are broken down into commodities and destinations in Appendices 6 and 7.

This book focuses mainly on the Middle East. The figures quoted above are evidence of a considerable increase in exports of Indian engineering goods to that buoyant market, to the point where, as Appendix 7 demonstrates, 'West Asia' has become the leading market.[21] But figures are virtually meaningless without an analysis of what lies behind them. This is not simply a question of breaking them down into commodities and destinations. An attempt must be made to recount the radical changes that have taken place in the last few years in Indian exporting methods and abilities. Until a few years ago Indian engineering exports to the region were simply exports of goods, at first of components and then with a growing

admixture of capital items. By the late 1970s more and more of them
formed part of a *project,* often Indian-led. The Indian construction firms
(many of them old-established private sector concerns, but also new
purpose-formed, public sector organizations) were active throughout
the region in civil engineering and mechanical erection projects, and
Indian engineering firms—consultants and manufacturers—were
making their presence felt in a number of turnkey projects. The
infrastructure to support this sort of overseas activity had been
considerably strengthened, and there is every indication that the
government and the private sector, having found that they are able
to compete successfully with firms from the developed countries, are
determined to increase their stake in the business of developing
other countries' economics. The initial construction boom in the
Gulf may now be over, but the Indians are looking further afield,
and they believe that they have the industrial diversity and muscle
to succeed elsewhere and in projects of greater complexity and size.
They reckon that their best chances lie in combining their strengths
with the complementary ones of other exporters. Their first preference as a partner was for the United Kingdom, but they are
becoming impatient with what they see as a distinct lack of enthusiasm
on the British side and are consequently looking elsewhere. They
have shown signs of settling for the Republic of Korea.[22] An Indo-
Korean combination could prove overwhelming, particularly in
civil engineering. It is a prospect that the British contracting industry
might do well to ponder.

Notes

[1] In fact India is probably the world's twentieth manufacturing nation,
or fifteenth in the non-communist world. The manufacturing industries'
'league table' for 1976, the latest year for which UN statistics are generally
available, is as follows:

Manufacturing Industries' Product (US\$ bn)

1	USA	405.0	7	UK	51.5
2	USSR*	268.4 (all industry)	8	Poland*	41.5 (all industry)
3	West Germany	178.5	9	East Germany*	37.7 (all industry, at 1975 prices)
4	Japan	169.1			
5	France	92.1	10	Canada	35.7
6	Italy	57.8 (includes mining and quarrying)	11	Brazil	30.8
			12	Spain	26.3 (1975)
			13	Netherlands	25.4

Manufacturing Industries' Product (US$ bn)—cont'd

14 Czechoslovakia*	24.3 (all industry)	23 Hungary*	9.7 (all industry)
15 Sweden	20.8	24 Finland	8.1
16 Belgium	20.1	25 Bulgaria*	7.9 (all industry)
17 Australia	17.0 (1975)	26 { South Africa	7.6
18 Mexico	14.5	{ Republic of Korea	7.6
19 India†	13.1	28 Argentina	7.4
20 { Austria	13.0	29 Turkey	7.3
{ Yugoslavia	13.0	30 Iran	6.9
22 Romania*‡	11.5 (all industry)		

* Centrally planned economy (CPE): accounting methods and exchange rate calculations not strictly comparable.

† Note remarks below, concerning the People's Republic of China.

‡ The source in this case is UN, *Yearbook of National Accounts Statistics 1977*.

Source: UN, *Monthly Statistical Bulletin*, May 1979.

India comes even lower in the total industrial production league (i.e. including mining and quarrying and electricity, gas, and water).

This table is unsatisfactory in a number of ways. First, it omits the People's Republic of China, for which the UN does not quote any figures. Second, it may give a misleading impression of the relative position of two groups of countries, the centrally planned economies (CPEs) and some of the South American countries, owing to the distortions caused by differences in accounting methods and enormous exchange rate variations respectively.

If we accept that China's GNP is roughly four times that of India (the 1978 edition of the *World Bank Atlas* puts it at US$ bn 290.16 (1975), 307.01 (1976), and 346.35 (1977), as opposed to US$ bn 82.4, 87.85, and 97.37 for the same years for India), it is a fairly safe assumption that China ranks above India in manufacturing industries production. India would, therefore, come twentieth world-wide, or fifteenth in the non-communist world.

[2] A 'large industrial' house is a firm with total assets of not less than Rs. 20 crore.

[3] India, *Draft Five Year Plan 1978–83* (1978), ch. 11.

[4] The *1978 World Bank Atlas* puts India at $150 for 1976.

[5] These figures are very approximate and are derived, with suitable adjustments to take account of the subsequent increase in population, from the 1971 census.

[6] A British government publication in January 1979 listed twenty-three such cases: Hong Kong, Singapore, Republic of Korea, Taiwan, Malaysia, Philippines, Thailand, India, Pakistan, Iran, Israel, Brazil, Argentina, Mexico, Spain, Portugal, Yugoslavia, Greece, Turkey, Malta, Poland, Romania, and Hungary. They were 'classified as newly-industrialising and

which supplied UK imports of not less than £10 million in 1977', which presumably rules out a few smaller economies exhibiting comparable characteristics. GB, Foreign and Commonwealth Office, *The Newly Industrialising Countries and the Adjustment Problem* (1979, Govt Economic Service Working Paper no. 18), p. iii.

[7] The Soviet Prime Minister, Mr Kosygin, was reported as describing this policy during his spring 1979 visit to India as 'unscientific and lopsided', a description to which the Indian Industry Minister, George Fernandes, took exception. (*Economic Times*, 12 May 1979.)

[8] The British government's attitude towards Indian industrialization became gradually less negative during the inter-war years. Indian cotton textiles, production of which had been greatly expanded during the First World War, were given some protection from 1930 onwards, but the protective tariffs were just as much a means of protecting British textiles in the Indian market against Japanese competition as of encouraging the domestic Indian textile industry, more so perhaps. M. Lipton and J. Firn, *The Erosion of a Relationship: India and Britain since 1960* (1976), ch. 4.

[9] This integrated mill, owned by the Tata subsidiary Tata Iron and Steel Company Ltd (TISCO), was founded in 1907. Its capacity was expanded from 1 to 2 million tonnes of crude steel per day in the late Fifties and it is now the only major Indian steel mill in the private sector. It is also the most consistently productive.

[10] It was the Second Five Year Plan (1956/7–1960/1) that really set India's heavy industrialization in train, with the establishment of the first three public sector steel plants at Durgapur, Bhilai, and Rourkela, with British, Soviet, and Federal German assistance respectively.

[11] The USSR helped India to establish new capacity in a number of fields, notably steel, heavy machine building, coal mining, thermal power, and drugs manufacturing.

[12] The 'core sector' consists of the following basic industries. (1) Metallurgical industries: ferro alloys; steel castings and forgings; special steels; non-ferrous metals and their alloys. (2) Boilers and steam generating plants. (3) Prime movers (other than electrical generators): industrial turbines; internal combustion engines. (4) Electrical equipment: equipment for transmission and distribution of electricity; electrical motors; electrical furnaces; X-ray equipment; electronic components and equipment. (5) Transportation: mechanized sailing vessels up to 1000 DWT; ship ancillaries; commercial vehicles. (6) Industrial machinery. (7) Machine tools. (8) Agricultural machinery: tractors and power tillers. (9) Earthmoving machinery. (10) Industrial instruments: indicating, recording, and regulating devices for pressure, temperature, rate of flow, weights, levels, and the like. (11) Scientific instruments. (12) Nitrogenous and phosphatic fertilizers. (13) Chemicals (other than fertilizers): inorganic heavy chemicals; organic heavy chemicals; fine chemicals, including photographic chemicals; synthetic resins and plastics; synthetic rubbers; man-made fibres; industrial explo-

sives; insecticides, fungicides, herbicides, and the like; synthetic detergents; miscellaneous chemicals (for industrial use only). (14) Drugs and pharmaceuticals. (15) Paper and pulp including paper products. (16) Automobile tyres and tubes. (17) Plate glass. (18) Ceramics: refractories; furnace lining bricks—acidic, basic, and neutral. (19) Cement products: Portland cement; asbestos cement.

Under the terms of the Foreign Exchange (Regulation) Act of 1973 (FERA) foreign investors are not permitted to hold more than 40 per cent of the equity of an Indian firm unless it employs sophisticated technology, is export oriented, or is within the core sector. In this last respect FERA refined existing regulations confining new foreign investment to the core industries.

[13] India has a wider range of consultancy services than any other developing country and leads the LDCs in the provision of turnkey services. Indian consultants are also gaining increasing acceptance in developed countries where their lower costs have enabled them to take on a considerable amount of subcontracting work. (Sanjaya Lall, 'Developing Countries as Exporters of Industrial Technology', *Research Policy*, 9/1 (1980.)

[14] The MRTPA was passed in 1969 and a Monopolies Commission was established in 1970.

[15] In May 1978 the government agreed to implement certain recommendations made by the Sondhi Committee, which had been set up in September 1976 to examine suggestions for the liberalization of imports of capital goods 'in order to promote dynamism and growth in the industrial sector'. In particular fourteen specified industries were to be permitted to invite global tenders for capital goods, and actual users of certain capital goods manufactured in India but deemed to receive sufficient protection from import duties could in future import them under Open General Licence (OGL). The fourteen industries were: fertilizers; newsprint and paper; basic drugs; basic technical materials for pesticides and weedicides; power generation, transmission, and distribution; mineral exploration, mining, and beneficiation; petroleum exploration and production; petrochemicals up to the stage of polymers; manufacture of professional grade electronic components; waste disposal recycling and effluent treatment projects and ecological engineering; materials handling projects at ports; sugar; cement and cement products (including asbestos); 100 per cent export-oriented industries.

Other significant forms of liberalization in the 1978/9 import policy were that actual users could henceforth import their requirements of raw materials, components, and spare parts under OGL, and automatic licences for imports of restricted raw materials and components were to be issued on the basis of 110 per cent of previous consumption (as opposed to 100 per cent).

[16] India, *Draft Five Year Plan 1978–83*, para. 3.90 (ii).

[17] India, *1978/9 Economic Survey*, p 57.

[18] *Economic Times*, 4 May 1979.

[19] The rate of increase slowed down in 1978/9, but it was nevertheless still continuing. According to the *Economic Times* of 8 May 1979 engineering exports grew by 5 per cent in 1978/9, a rate of growth that was expected to be maintained in 1979/80.

[20] *Economic Times*, 15 Nov. 1978.

[21] This lead, understandably, is forecast to diminish as other regional markets are built up and the Middle East development boom slows down.

[22] In a sense they already have done, though probably not exclusively. On 3 Apr. 1979 the Association of Indian Engineering Industry signed an agreement with the Federation of Korean Industries for close 'cooperation and collaboration' designed to give 'unmatched competition' to other countries for third country projects (*Economic Times*, 4 Apr. 1979).

2

Industrial Exports

THIS chapter examines three aspects of Indian industrial exports: hardware (the 'engineering goods' of Indian trade statistics), construction, and consultancy services. Its object is to identify the types of goods and construction activity and the forms of consultancy service in which Indian firms have done most business abroad in recent years, so as to build up a picture of Indian capabilities in other developing countries in general and the Middle East in particular.

Hardware

Indian trade statistics divide engineering exports into four main categories: (i) capital goods; (ii) primarily steel and pig iron based items; (iii) non-ferrous products; and (iv) consumer durables. This categorization leads to some anomalies. 'Complete vehicles', for instance, count as capital goods, whereas 'auto parts' and 'diesel engines and compressors' are regarded as consumer durables. The dividing line between capital goods and steel and iron based items in also a trifle difficult to discern, with 'wires and cables' in the former and 'mild steel wire products' and 'wire ropes' in the latter. In general capital goods are substantial completed investment goods; steel and iron based items are ferrous intermediate goods; and non-ferrous goods are self-explanatory. Consumer durables are mainly small engineering goods, including electronics and hand tools. The term 'consumer durable' has rather different connotations for the average Western reader. But, as this is a book about Indian exports, it would be wise to stick to Indian terminology.[1]

India's principal capital goods exports in the 1970s consisted of fabricated steel structures; transmission towers and poles; machine tools; textile and other miscellaneous machinery; electrical control-gear and switchgear; electrical transformers; aluminium conductor cables; insulated cables; buses and lorries; chassis with engines;

13

railway wagons; railway locomotives; railway wagon components; and coastal vessels and ships. Each of these categories notched up overseas sales of more than Rs. 2.5 crore in 1976/7. Certain other capital goods sold well in one or two markets, including pulp and paper mill, sugar mill and oil mill machinery, electrical generators, and mechanical handling equipment.

Primarily steel and pig iron based categories that also recorded export sales of more than Rs. 2.5 crore in 1976/7 were bright steel bars; bolts and nuts; cast iron pipes and fittings; steel furniture; steel pipes and tubes; wire ropes; wire netting; wire nails, needles and pins; and builders' hardware. On the same basis the best selling non-ferrous exports were aluminium ingots and EPNS ware. And the most successful consumer durables were hand, small, and cutting tools; pressure oil lamps and stoves; diesel engines, parts, and pumpsets; mechanical pumps; air conditioners and refrigerators; storage batteries; electrical accessories; electric fans and parts; radios and parts; automobile parts; complete bicycles and bicycle parts (Appendix 6 below).

These best-selling lines give a good indication of the wide variety of Indian engineering exports and thus of the industries that supply them. The industries themselves spread across of wide spectrum of ownership and scale, from the big public sector plants that turn out many of the capital and intermediate goods, to privately owned factories in the small-scale sector producing items such as hand tools and bicycles.[2]

The Middle East is India's best market for engineering exports. It took 36 per cent of them in 1976/7 and nearly 36 per cent in 1977/8. Southeast Asia follows, with 21 per cent and 25 per cent respectively. (See Appendix 7.) As is only to be expected, construction materials and intermediates sold well in the Middle East during the post oil price-rise boom. Certain capital goods, particularly transmission line towers and electrical switchgear, also did well. These were, in general, the goods that experienced the highest increase in sales over the three years in question. For instance, exports of bright steel bars tripled, from Rs. 2.5 crore to Rs. 9.1 crore. Cast iron pipes and fittings quadrupled, from Rs. 4.2 crore to Rs. 18.6 crore. Transmission line towers almost doubled, from Rs. 5.1 crore to Rs. 9.0 crore. Indeed most of the Indian exports associated with a boom in construction and establishment of utilities, such as the oil-rich countries of the Middle East have been experiencing since 1974, doubled, or more than doubled, in value over the three years concerned. (In real terms the increases were almost as striking, since the wholesale price indices for all commodities and manufactured products rose from 174.9 and 168.8 in 1974/5 to only 176.6 and 175.2 in 1976/7 respectively.)[3]

It is likely that demand in the Middle East for construction materials and intermediates, and the types of capital goods associated with the creation of a basic infrastructure, such as electric power equipment, will flatten or even fall in the next few years as the construction boom peters out, at least in the Gulf. Indian exporters will then have to look more to the area's efforts to build up its industrial base for their business. The focus of these efforts will be on oil refining and petrochemicals. Indian industry is well equipped to supply many of the necessary hydrocarbon processing inputs, both plant and intermediate in which India has built up a high degree of self-sufficiency (99 per cent in electrical equipment for petrochemical and fertilizer plants, 92 per cent in instrumentation and control valves, 88 per cent in mechanical and process equipment including alloy steel, low temperature steel, and titanium and monel).[4]

So much for the nature, value, and destination of Indian hardware. But what is it like? Is it primitive and out of date? What about quality?

These are loaded and difficult questions. One answer--it may be the best one—is simply to quote the record. Exports of Indian engineering goods rose (see Appendix 4) more than sevenfold from 1968/9 to 1977/8, from Rs. 84.4 core to Rs. 650 crore. Quite a bit of this was of course accounted for by inflation, but in volume terms the story is still impressive, as Appendix 8 shows. Exports of manufactures of metals more than tripled. Those of machinery and transport equipment quadrupled. And exports of non-ferrous metals rose nearly threefold. Increases of this order have continued, but more recent volume indices were at the time of writing not available. The importers must have been reasonably satisfied for growth rates of this order to have been achieved. Even iron and steel, after some lean years in the mid-1970s, were more than holding their own despite the general drop in world demand.

Few Indian designs incorporate the very latest technology. But most of it is the result of careful choice from its original developers in the industrialized countries of both East and West, followed by adaptation and modification to suit Indian conditions from operating experience gained in those conditions. Some of the technology is also home-brewed Indian from its inception, and a good deal is an amalgam of both. Its suitability for Indian conditions makes it *a priori* suitable for conditions in many other developing countries, and in that sense it is 'appropriate' technology.

There can be no satisfactory proof. But an example of this 'tropicalization' of imported technology might serve to illuminate it:

the Tata Engineering and Locomotive Company (TELCO) five-ton truck. This is based on a 1954 Mercedes model which was originally, under the terms of a 15-year collaboration agreement, assembled in India from German-made parts. Gradually TELCO took over manufacture itself, with the result that now a TELCO truck is more than 98 per cent made in India. More important, it is a very different vehicle from the original 1954 model. Its frame, suspension, axles, brakes, and gearbox are all much stronger. It has a more powerful and more economical engine, designed by TELCO. These changes were introduced to suit Indian conditions, and this vehicle frequently outsells its present-day German cousin in other developing countries. That is not to say that it is a *better* truck—just different and more 'appropriate' for conditions in many LDCs.[5]

The same can probably be said of a great many Indian capital goods and consumer durables. Indian electrical power equipment, for instance, is designed to run in less than ideal conditions; thermal boilers must be capable of burning coal with a high ash content and switchgear and generators must be able to go on working even if maintenance procedures are delayed or skimped. Electronic equipment has been redesigned so as to operate in dusty conditions, and the technology for the manufacture of citric acid has been adapted so as to use cane molasses as the raw material rather than beet sugar. And in some skills and technologies India has an edge over many developed countries, including Britain. Indian welding is generally of a very high standard (with low labour costs Indian welders can afford to take their time) and, in process plant, Indian layered vessel and compressor technology is well up to the highest world standards. The finish may not be always up to the highest Western standards— and frequently is not—but the equipment itself is sturdy and well proven.[6]

Construction

India has a large construction industry, contributing about Rs. 4,600 crore to GDP in 1977/8. It is rather more than one-third the size of manufacturing industry in GDP terms,[7] and this relatively high proportion is reflected in India's comparative international strength in construction.[8]

The industry has grown up with the major expansion of India's manufacturing industry, infrastructure, and towns since Independence. Until fairly recently it was a largely private sector affair. But during the 1970s both the central government and the state governments set up their own organizations to work on public projects. Most of the larger firms have ventured into the overseas market;

indeed some of those in the public sector, for example Engineering Projects (India) Ltd (EPI) and Projects and Equipment Corporation Ltd (PEC), were set up in order to undertake large overseas projects. The private sector has also to a certain extent reorganized itself to take advantage of overseas work, by regrouping into consortia and setting up local joint-venture operations abroad. Siporex India Ltd is an example of the first (it is a consortium of eight construction companies based in and around Poona), and Gammon Midest, which is based in the UAE, is an example of the second. (It is 50 per cent owned by Gammon (India) Ltd.)

Even a most cursory tour of some of India's newer industrial and infrastructural facilities will give a visitor a good impression of the scope and scale of the Indian construction industry. Enormous bridges and dams, including the world's longest river bridge (5.5 km, at Patna) and the world's longest and—until recently—highest dams (nearly 5 km at Hirakud, and 226 m at Bhakra, respectively), have been built or are being built all over the country. New roads have been pushed into the most inhospitable places, particularly in the Himalayas,[9] and new railways are still being built (in contrast to what is happening in most Western countries, where many railways are being pulled up). New factories and plant have sprung up in the major conurbations (and, in the case of many of the refineries, petrochemical plants and nuclear installations, a long way outside them) and high-rise buildings are clustered together in Indian Manhattans, particularly in Bombay. Virtually all this construction and mechanical erection has been done by Indian firms. By 1978 some twenty-five of them were at work outside India, all of them firms whose whole experience had been gained from working in a developing country, with all which that so often implies concerning shortages of materials, poor communications, under-trained work-forces, and extremes of climatic and other physical conditions.

Indian construction companies are at work on projects throughout the Middle East, both as lead contractors and subcontractors. Their scope seems to be as wide as it is in India. Indian companies have won turnkey contracts in housing and public building; sewerage and water supply; road, airport, and dam building; and in more specialized civil construction such as grain storage silos. They have also been retained as subcontractors in the same fields, and, particularly, in mechanical erection in fields such as desalination and petrochemical plant. Manufacturers of electrical plant and equipment such as Bharat Heavy Electricals Ltd (BHEL) and Kamani Engineering generally act as their own mechanical erectors in the various turnkey projects which they have won, and Kamani and other firms have also won line stringing subcontracts.

Project exports, which combine in one package both the goods themselves and their erection or incorporation in some other structure or installation, accounted during the late 1970s for a steadily increasing share of Indian engineering exports to the Middle East. Turnkey projects earned India about Rs. 250 crore in 1977/8, or almost one-third of total engineering exports to the region, with further projects worth a further Rs. 675 crore under way in February 1979.[10]

Consultancy

It is difficult to generalize about Indian consultancy organizations. Some, like Metallurgical and Engineering Consultants (India) Ltd (MECON) and M.N. Dastur and Co. (Dasturco) are major concerns, with some hundreds of engineers and other qualified staff, while others are firms employing but two or three people. In all they employ more than 15,000 qualified staff. Some have been consultants pure and simple from the outset (Dasturco and the National Industrial Development Corporation (NIDC), for instance), while others such as MECON have grown out of the design departments of, for the most part, nationalized industries (in this case steel). Some are part of a multinational concern, such as Powergas India Ltd, and others are primarily manufacturers, such as BHEL. Nearly all the firms offering their services overseas are members of the Federation of Indian Export Organizations (FIEO).[11]

Indian consultancy firms offer general consultancy services in three main areas:

(i) *Economic:* e.g. regional and area development studies, market surveys, economic appraisal;

(ii) *Management:* e.g. manpower planning, computerization, material management, work study, operation research, structure modernization;

(iii) *Management of construction and operation:* e.g. programming, scheduling and progressing, supervision and inspection, erection, equipment supplies, and commissioning.

Most FIEO consultancy firms operate, according to their particular specialization, in area (iii). Only a few cover areas (i) and (ii).[12]

The specialized firms provide the whole range of services furnished by their opposite numbers in developed countries, such as plan formulations, project reports, basic engineering, plant design and detailed engineering, construction management and start-up services, and operational management consultancy services. The range of their specializations reflects the broad spread of Indian industry.

They provide their services to metallurgical plants (iron and steel and non-ferrous), process plans (e.g. sugar, cement, and chemicals), pulp and paper, textiles and synthetic fibres, agricultural inputs, food processing, engineering and capital goods, and oil refineries and petrochemicals. They also of course provide the whole range of infrastructure and other civil engineering services such as power generation (nuclear, thermal, and hydro), transmission and distribution, railways, roads and bridges, water supply, drainage and sewerage, irrigation and flood control, town planning and architecture, and buildings and structures.[13]

All these skills and specializations have been acquired and put into practice within the framework of a developing country. Few, if any, of India's consultancy firms existed at the time of Independence. They grew up with the industrialization that has taken place in the last thirty years, at first learning from it through subcontracts to overseas firms, but later planning and managing it themselves. Their collective experience is now considerable, and since the late 1960s they have been putting it at the disposal of other developing countries, both directly and by means of subcontracts to consultants from developed countries. And they have been increasingly retained by the main international development agencies.[14]

Notes

[1] The main categories are as follows.

A. *Capital goods:* industrial plant and machinery; electric power machinery and switchgear; transmission line towers and poles; steel structures (fabricated); wires and cables; wagons and coaches; coastal vessels and ships; complete vehicles; machine tools.

B. *Primarily steel and pig iron based items:* steel pipes and tubes; bright bars; ferrous holloware; mild steel wire products; industrial fasteners; high carbon wire products (wire ropes); sanitary castings; industrial castings; forgings; steel products not otherwise specified.

C. *Non-ferrous products:* aluminium products; EPNS ware; non-ferrous products (other than aluminium).

D. *Consumer durables:* auto parts; bicycles and parts; hand, small and cutting tools; diesel engines and compressors; mechanical pumps; heating and cooling equipment; electric fans and parts; electronics; batteries; sewing machines; knitting machines; electric manufactures not otherwise stated; miscellaneous manufactured articles.

These headings are of course further subdivided. The subdivisions reveal further anomalies. Agricultural implements are, for instance, B.10. But tractors are A.1. Cranes and lifts are A.4 and ball bearings are D.13.

[2] There are of course also factories in the large-scale sector producing bicycles. They are among India's most successful engineering enterprises. Bicycle spares are, however, reserved for the small-scale sector.

[3] On a base of 100 for 1970/1, according to H. L. Chandhok's *Wholesale Price Statistics 1947–1978* (1979).

[4] More specifically, India can manufacture the following hydrocarbon processing equipment:

Fabricated equipment: (i) Fabricated equipment, reaction vessels, storage vessels, columns, heat exchangers up to 200 tonnes in weight and using rolled plates up to 140 mm thick; (ii) Multilayer vessels with wall thickness in excess of 140 mm; (iii) Construction material including boiler quality steel, alloy and high alloy steel, high tensile steel, carbon steel, all varieties of stainless steel and special materials including copper, aluminium, brass, nickel, and special alloys such as monel; (iv) Clad columns, different types of dishes including multilayer petals; (v) Major equipment including carbon dioxide absorbers, synthesis reactors for urea, multitube reactors (up to 10,000 tubes), 106 metre columns erected vertically in three pieces; (vi) 55 mm thick stainless steel storage vessels for ethylene.

Rotating equipment: (vii) Drive turbines up to 4,000 BHP; (viii) Centrifugal compressors for handling up to 350,000 m^3/hr and discharging up to pressures 350 kg/cm^2; (ix) Reciprocating compressors, process and water service pumps, fire fighting pumps, vacuum pumps, etc.

[5] *New Scientist,* 5 Oct. 1978. In fact, from the point of view of suitability for European conditions, the Tata lorry could be said to be inferior to its German cousin, in that it incorporates none of the Mercedes design changes made since 1954, most of which relate to safety, comfort, and speed. But that is not the point.

[6] These are judgements I am not qualified to make. But they reflect the opinions of certain British consulting engineers with considerable experience of both the British and Indian engineering industries. Also, BHEL claims to be a world leader in fluidized bed boiler technology.

[7] Out of total 1977/8 GDP at factor cost (current prices) of Rs. 78,244 crore, manufacturing and construction contributed Rs. 12,818 crore and Rs. 4,603 crore, or 16.4 per cent and 5.9 per cent respectively, according to an (Indian) Central Statistical Office press note of 8 Jan. 1979.

[8] Fourteenth in the non-communist world in 1976. Nineteenth in the whole world. (UN, *Monthly Bulletin of Statistics,* May 1979.)

[9] Where India can claim another world record, for the highest motor road, between Manali and Leh, which runs at an average height of just under 14,000 ft and crosses three passes, the highest of which is nearly 18,000 ft.

[10] *Economic Times,* 15 Feb. 1979.

[11] The FIEO, of Allahabad Bank Building, 17 Parliament Street, New Delhi 110001, publishes a useful directory of these fifty firms.

[12] The NIDC is prominent under (i), and Tata Consultancy Services under (ii).

[13] I am indebted to Mr Kan Mariwalla, the Chairman and Managing Director of the NIDC, for this résumé.

[14] In particular, IBRD, IDA, UNIDO, ESCAP, ECLA, and ADB.

3

Overseas Projects and Consultancies

WE have seen in the previous chapter how a major share of India's exports of engineering goods forms part of wider project sales and how a number of India's larger construction companies have started to take on overseas contracts in recent years. This chapter will be concerned with some of these projects,[1] which can thus serve to illustrate the extent to which Indian firms have, in the space of only five or six years, blossomed forth into international operations, after histories in most cases of purely domestic activity. The chapter will also examine the overseas record of India's consultancy organizations, which, though in many cases with a rather longer history of overseas assignments, have also expanded this aspect of their work in the last few years. This has resulted partly from the natural association of Indian consultants with Indian projects overseas and partly from their own independent efforts to win overseas work.

The Indian contracting presence in the Middle East is most visible in the form of large construction projects in which the lead contract is held by an Indian firm, with most of the specialized subcontracts let to other Indian firms, with all that that implies in terms of large numbers of migrant Indian workers. Projects of this sort are generally in housing and other forms of civil construction and in electrification. But, just as important from the point of view of India's balance of payments, and perhaps more valuable from the point of view of the opportunities which they provide of learning from the experience of foreign firms with a longer tradition of overseas work, are the subcontracts—in civil works, mechanical erection, and so on.

The Indian embassies in Iraq, Kuwait, Libya, Saudi Arabia, and the United Arab Emirates kindly prepared lists of major projects, and, in some cases, joint ventures, in the countries to which they were accredited. These are reproduced at Appendices 20 to 24 below.

Joint Ventures

There are also projects that are the result of Indian overseas investment in the form of joint ventures, in which the Indian share of the
investment had, until recently, to take the form of plant or equipment.[2] Most of these joint ventures are in Southeast Asia and Africa,
probably because the 'local' partner was himself an expatriate
Indian or national of Indian origin,[3] often with family connections
with the 'genuinely' Indian investor. But towards the end of the
1970s Indians began to turn their attention also to the Middle East
for joint ventures in a variety of small industrial concerns in light
engineering and the manufacture of domestic electrical equipment.[4]

Outward Indian investment of this sort is not confined to the
private sector. Hindustan Machine Tools (HMT), for instance, has
established itself in the Philippines, Sri Lanka, Nigeria, and Kenya
in this way. In the Kenyan case the Kenyan Industrial and Commercial Development Corporation (ICDC) joined with HMT in
1978 to set up a Rs. 4 crore plant to manufacture machine tools.
HMT holds 25 per cent of the equity (the value of the Indian
equipment, based on East European technology).

Kenya and its ICDC also provide a convenient example of a joint
venture in a more conventional field. JK Synthetics, a private sector
organization with a number of overseas links, set up a Rs. 8.5 crore,
5 tonne per day, nylon filament plant in 1978. Each side holds 49
per cent of the equity, with the 2 per cent balance held privately.
Similar mills have been established in recent years in Southeast Asia
by firms such as Gwalior Rayons (part of the Birla group) and
Lakshmi Textiles.

Construction

Civil and Structural Engineering

Nearly all India's major construction companies have taken advantage of the Middle Eastern building boom, often as subcontractors
but also as turnkey operators offering a complete design and
construction package. At least twenty-five of them[5] were at work on
building contracts in and around the Gulf in 1978, mostly in the
private sector. The most prominent were Engineering Construction
Corporation (ECC), Siporex, Continental Construction, Gammon
(India), Shah Construction, B. G. Shirke, and Shapoorji Pallonji. The
public sector was represented principally by EPI and the National
Buildings Construction Corporation Ltd (NBCC). Other public
sector firms included the International Airports Authority of India
(IAAI), the Indian Road Construction Corporation Ltd (IRCC)

and Bridge and Roof Co. (India) Ltd, a subsidiary of Balmer Lawrie which was itself also active overseas. The contracts that these and other firms have won are too numerous to list comprehensively, but an idea of their variety can be gained from the examples referred to in the next few paragraphs.

In the private sector ECC, a subsidiary of Larsen & Toubro, won a Rs. 26 crore subcontract to a Japanese firm to build a new terminal for Abu Dhabi international airport late in 1976, and a year later, with its parent company, was awarded a Rs. 1.6 crore turnkey contract for a dairy in South Yemen. The firm also won a Rs. 10 crore subcontract to erect a natural gas liquefaction plant at Doha in Qatar. Continental Construction gained a Rs. 71 crore contract in September 1977 to build a dam at Wadi Ghan in Libya, against German, French, and Turkish competition, with Texmaco (a Birla-owned engineering firm) designing and manufacturing the mechanical equipment. Shah Construction was awarded contracts for the construction of a liquid sulphur terminal at Basrah, Iraq (against competition from German contractors) and of two bridges (once more against German competition), also in Iraq. The firm also tendered successfully for the construction of a wholesale market at Doha. Shapoorji Pallonji completed the Sultan of Oman's new palace at Muscat in late 1978. Siporex had at the same time nearly completed a Rs. 60 crore contract for 1,710 houses at Dubai and had other contracts (in Saudi Arabia, Kuwait, and South Yemen), together worth a further Rs. 37 crore. With a Saudi Arabian partner it had also set up a joint venture company to manufacture prefabricated buildings in Saudi Arabia.

Gammon (India) Ltd (GIL) took on a sub-contract to BHEL for civil works for the Tripoli West power station project in 1977. It was also engaged on a Rs. 5 crore mechanical erection subcontract to erect a $5 \times 13,000$ m³pd desalination plant at Jebel Ali near Dubai (Sumitomo Heavy Industries was the main contractor). This assignment, which might perhaps serve as a model of its type, was GIL's first overseas mechanical job. Work started in February 1978 and was expected to be completed, ahead of schedule, in March 1980. The labour force, all from India, consisted of 227 skilled men and 35 professional staff. Their task was to erect 8,900 tonnes of structural steel and piping, all the equipment, and all the electricals and instrumentation. Much of this involved plate and tube work requiring a very high degree of skill of the sort at which Indian fitters excel, and which Sumitomo seemed happy to acknowledge.[6]

Much the largest Indian construction job in the Middle East is the Ardiya Project just outside Kuwait, a joint venture between Pacific Consultants International of Japan (architects and consultants) and EPI. Indeed EPI maintained in 1978 that it was the biggest single housing project under construction in the world. The contract's value was $280.4 million. It involved the construction of 3,317 houses, 10 mosques, a police station, a shopping centre, and so on; everything in fact for a self-contained dormitory town with a population of about 26,000. The houses were intended for lower income groups. In Kuwaiti circumstances this still meant that each would have up to four bedrooms, two sitting rooms, a garage, and airconditioning.

Construction was to have been completed by the end of 1979, but the project got off to a bad start, and completion was not expected until September 1980. The Kuwaiti National Housing Authority (the client) was said at one stage to be imposing a stiff daily penalty on EPI, but the contract was later renegotiated. The problems seem to have been that EPI had never before handled such a big job; that insufficient Indian labour was brought into Kuwait; and that the National Housing Authority, again probably because of inexperience, imposed unnecessarily strict quality and standards controls.

It was also reported[7] that some of the subcontractors had lured EPI's (Indian) labour force away with promises of higher pay and better conditions, one result of which was that those who remained went on strike with a demand for parity. The strike broke when its organizers were sent home to India, after which the project picked up momentum.

EPI's procurement policy is to obtain as much material and equipment from India as possible, other things being equal. In the case of the Ardiya project this meant in practice that most of the materials and about half the equipment and machinery were Indian, but most of the plant (i.e. block-making machinery etc.) was from West Germany. Some, including earth moving and tar melting equipment, was British.

EPI's problems at Ardiya do not seem to have affected its ability to go on winning contracts. The total value of its overseas projects under implementation in March 1979 was $666 million, $194 million of which was for contracts in Iraq, including two grain silos (worth $107 million), a water research centre ($18.9 million), and the expansion of a television station as associate contractor with Mitsubishi ($16.46 million). It was also building a $98 million army camp in Kuwait, where it had earlier completed a $3.5 million airport extension.[8] Other big construction firms such as Continental Construction, Bridge and Roof, Shah Construction, and Som Dutt were also heavily involved in Iraq.

Much of the NBCC's overseas activity was centred on two airport projects in Libya, at Ghat and Brak, which it was building in association with the International Airports Authority of India (IAAI). The company was also building a township at Ghat (300 houses and a 120-bed hospital), a 1,000-house township at Beniwalid, and a 22-km road at Ghat. The total value of these Libyan contracts, which were won on a negotiated basis as the result of a promotional exercise mounted by the Indian government, was Rs. 150 crore. The NBCC's other major overseas contracts at the time of writing were both in Iraq: two flyovers near Baghdad airport ($6 million) and a $6-million new building complex for Baghdad University.

Road building is often incorporated in wider civil engineering projects, as for example the 22-km road which EPI built as part of the Ghat airport project. But a number of road building contracts have also been let in their own right in the Middle East, and to take advantage of this the government of India set up a new public sector organization under the aegis of the Ministry of Shipping and Transport in December 1976. This is the Indian Road Construction Corporation Ltd (IRCC). The Corporation was by 1978 registered in Saudi Arabia, Iraq, Libya, North Yemen, Malaysia, and Thailand, and was at work on two contracts, in Libya and Iraq, worth Rs. 13 crore and Rs. 10 crore respectively. The first was for 73 km of road and the second for a bridge and approach roads. It was negotiating with Libya late in 1978 for a further two contracts for 1,300 km of roads, together worth Rs. 150 crore. The Corporation has close links with the long-established paramilitary Border Roads Organization from which it is able to draw experienced and disciplined engineers and skilled workers, many of whom were at work in Libya and Iraq. (The Border Roads Organization builds and maintains roads in India's frontier regions, almost all of which consist either of mountains, desert, or rain forest, and is probably therefore as experienced as any organization in the world in building roads in difficult and inhospitable country.)

Plant

Indian engineering firms have done a useful turnkey trade in a good many types of industrial and process plant. In textile mill machinery, for instance, a consortium of manufacturers won a Rs. 7.72 crore contract in 1977 to set up a 37,000 spindle cotton spinning mill in Tanzania. In sugar mill machinery Walchandnagar Industries Ltd contracted to supply Tanzania with a complete sugar mill, also in 1977, for Rs. 30.26 crore.[9] Both were examples of true turnkey projects, including provision for training. There have been numerous examples of similar but smaller contracts, and some rather surprising ones, such as Larsen & Toubro's in 1978 to supply and, initially, run a complete dairy in the Yemen Arab Republic for Rs. 1.45 crore.

Hindustan Machine Tools Ltd (HMT) won a Rs. 10 crore contract in 1978 to supply a plant to manufacture gas meters and regulators in Algeria, beating (among others) Vickers Ltd of the UK on price despite the more advanced technology offered by the latter. The evidence is scanty, but this could have been an example of a developing country importer accepting the Indian thesis of the 'appropriateness' of its technology in a field in which the latest is almost always regarded as the best.

EPI's projects were not exclusively in civil and structural engineering. As at March 1979 EPI was involved in three industrial plant projects: the two grain silo complexes in Iraq together worth $107 million and a $1.5 million water treatment plant in Thailand. It had earlier completed a number of comparable projects (e.g. a centre for training in mechanical skills worth $12.52 million and a water supply project worth $19.9 million, both in Iraq).

Power and Telecommunications

Bharat Heavy Electricals Ltd (BHEL), a public sector undertaking set up during the Fifties and Sixties with assistance from the United States, the Soviet Union, Czechoslovakia, and the United Kingdom, manufactures a comprehensive range of heavy electrical equipment (generators, steam and hydro turbines, boilers, switchgear, cables, transformers, motors, etc). Employing 56,000 people, it was by 1977 India's largest engineering company, and in capacity terms (up to 6,000 MW a year) quite big by world standards—roughly on a par with GEC (UK),[10] with an exportable surplus of about 1,000 MW a year. Its technology is a mixture of inherited and adapted designs, with a growing admixture of new technology from its own R & D division. The company entered into an agreement with Kraftwerk Union (KWU) in 1978 in order to acquire updated technology that would, among other things, enable it to manufacture larger turbosets of up to 1,000 MW. Throughout 1978 and the first half of 1979 it was also trying to conclude an agreement, for the acquisition of even more advanced technology, with Siemens. At the time of writing this effort was stuck in a bureaucratic log-jam, with the Committee of Secretaries[11] opposing the proposed link. The issues were complex—part political, part economic, and part technical. They are examined further in chapter 6 below.

From small beginnings, mainly of boilers to Malaysia, BHEL rapidly increased the value and volume of its exports, which were worth some $200 million in 1976/7. The company's overseas business ranged from supplies of generation, transmission, and distribution equipment to major turnkey projects. The first of these was won in 1977 and involved the enlargement of Tripoli West power station. Under the terms of this Rs. 96 crore contract, won in competition against bids from West Germany, Switzerland, France, Japan, and the UK, BHEL was to design, manufacture, ship, erect, commission, and, for four years, operate and maintain the additional 240 MW generating capacity (2 × 120) and infrastructures. At 565 MW the enlarged station was to be the biggest in North Africa. This contract was reported to be running six months late by the end of 1978[12] but was nevertheless followed up by a request from the Electricity Corporation of Libya to undertake the rehabilitation of parts of the original (French-equipped) power station. At the time of writing BHEL was negotiating for a much larger turnkey project in Libya, a 4 × 120 MW generating station with desalination. Interestingly the Libyans had specified KWU designs for this job, an early vindication of the KWU collaboration.

Also in 1977 BHEL won the Saudi Arabian contract, for the electrification of Wadi Jizan, which forms the subject of the introduction to this book. To recapitulate briefly: BHEL was, at the time of writing, building on a greenfield[13] site a 6 × 7 MW diesel generating station and housing complex, and was installing all the transmission and distribution equipment to take the power to about 8,000 consumers in 900 sq km of Wadi Jizan. The contract was won in interesting circumstances. The Saudis had earlier rejected bids from Western companies, on the grounds that they were both concerted and extortionate, and had instead invited four developing countries (India, Taiwan, the Republic of Korea, and Pakistan) to submit tenders. BHEL won, but one of the conditions was that its disaggregated prices had to be lower—that is, in all the constituent parts of the quotation—than those submitted by the 'extortionate' Western lowest bidder, as well as overall.

The Wadi Jizan project was a good test of BHEL's ingenuity. The site had absolutely no services of any kind. Before work could start wells had to be sunk; and, there being no telephone links with Jeddah, 800 km to the north, BHEL had to negotiate permission from the Saudi authorities to operate a wireless link. Jizan is on the YAR frontier, a sensitive area, and permission was not readily granted. Heavy equipment had to be landed on the beach, and, almost throughout the year, work has to stop during the middle hours of the day owing to the near-perennial midday sandstorm (it goes on at night to compensate).

Malaysia is one of BHEL's steadiest markets, mainly for boilers but also for transmission and distribution equipment. By early 1979 the company had supplied boilers there amounting to 870 MW, and total orders amounted to 1,110 MW, which, BHEL claimed, accounted for 80 per cent of Malaysia's thermal capacity.[14] Indeed the Malaysian authorities had by March 1979 placed five consecutive orders with BHEL, to the exclusion of all other suppliers, which says something for their confidence in BHEL's products. And in 1976 the company supplied ten hydro generators with a total output of 544 MW to two power stations in New Zealand (2 × 60 and 8 × 53 MW vertical shaft). In this last case BHEL benefited from a 20 per cent GSP preference, but nevertheless overcame the psychological barriers existing in the minds of most governments in developed countries concerning the purchase of vital capital plant from a developing country.

Both public and private sector concerns are involved in exporting transmission equipment. Hindustan Cables Ltd (public sector), which manufactures a wide range of cables, had export orders worth more than Rs. 10 crore on hand in 1977 and others worth a further Rs. 10 crore under negotiation. The destinations were Fiji, Kenya, Malaysia, Nigeria, Oman (and Muscat), Tonga, and Turkey. Kamani Engineering Corporation (private sector) had by 1978 built up a major export business and claimed to be the world's second largest exporter of transmission towers. Its overseas sales were nearly all through turnkey contracts and the orders it chalked up in 1977 were worth more than Rs. 100 crore. In Libya alone it had put up more than 1,200 km of transmission line (towers and high tension transmission cable). Its average annual work load by 1978 was 1,200 km, and it was equipped to undertake at least twelve major turnkey operations simultaneously (worldwide). Its 1978 limit was 500 KV equipment; work in its R & D wing was directed to raising the limit to 1,000 KV. Some 60 per cent of the materials used in the company's overseas projects were of Indian origin. Its main markets were Libya and Iran.

A number of other private sector firms such as Crompton Greaves, Inistrumentation (India) Ltd and Tata,[15] were regularly exporting a wide variety of electrical equipment, on a product and turnkey basis. Kamani's success was by no means exceptional. And, in the related field of telecommunications, the public sector Indian Telephone Industries (ITI) has carried out a number of turnkey jobs in Jordan, the UAE, and Oman, the Omani one being a Rs. 2 crore project for 3,000 subscriber connections completed in 1978.

Consultancies

We have seen in chapter 2 how India has developed a wide range of consultancy services, with many of the firms concerned exporting their skills in design, supervision, management, economic planning, and so on. Members of the Federation of Indian Export Organizations (FIEO) earned fees of Rs. 9.47 crore in foreign currency in 1977/8 in this way.[16] In the remainder of this chapter we shall see something of the work which they have been doing. It must be emphasized that this is merely a small selection. It is by no means comprehensive.

In the public sector the oldest firm, set up as a pioneer in 1954, is the National Industrial Development Corporation (NIDC), which specializes in industrial and economic development planning but is also equipped to provide total turnkey services for industrial projects. Engineers India Ltd (EIL) specializes in petrochemicals, and the specializations of Metallurgical and Engineering Consultants (India) Ltd (MECON), Water and Power Development Consultancy Services Ltd (WAPCOS), and Rail India Technical and Economic Services Ltd (RITES) need no further elucidation. Some of the big public sector corporations encountered above in the context of power and civil engineering, such as BHEL and EPI, also have consultancy wings, as does HMT which is otherwise primarily a manufacturer. Some research organizations, like the Central Machine Tool Institute (CMTI), also provide consultancy services.

The pioneer firm in the private sector, established in 1955, is M.N. Dastur and Co. (Dasturco), which specializes in steel. Other important firms in the private sector include Development Consultants Pvt Ltd, M.M. Suri and Associates, Consulting Engineering Services Ltd (CES), Birla Consultancy Pvt Ltd, Kirloskar Consultants, Tata Consulting Engineers (TCE), and Tata Consultancy Services (TCS). None of them has any rigid specialization apart from TCE and CES, which seem to be particularly active in power and infrastructure respectively, and TCS which specializes in management and data processing.

Steel

Dasturco's assignments have been virtually global in geographical spread. In the last ten years or so it has been involved with projects in twenty-six different countries[17] and with at least three international organizations.[18] These assignments have ranged from feasibility reports to responsibility for major turnkey contracts. The most impressive of the more recent ones is the Misurata iron and steel project in Libya, won in 1978. Dasturco was the principal consultant, responsible for the design and engineering of the whole complex of this greenfield plant. Stage 1 was to be for a capacity of 500,000 tpy, followed by an expansion to 5 million tpy. Under the terms of its contract Dasturco was also to provide general supervisory services for infrastructures, be responsible for the management of construction and erection, commissioning and start-up, and assist with recruitment and training of operating personnel.

MECON had among other things prepared feasibility studies for sponge iron and steel plants in Bangladesh, Singapore, and the UAE and was charged in 1977 by the Nigerian government with the installation of two 1 million tpy integrated steel plants. Earlier NIDC, in an untypical contract, had the overall consultancy for a small steel melting and billet casting plant in Tripoli.

Petroleum and Petrochemicals

EIL has done business in Algeria, Iran, Iraq, the Somali Republic, Sri Lanka, Syria, and the UAE. Its activities have ranged from subcontracts (examples include engineering, procurement, and construction supervision of offsites and utilities for Kellogg's fertilizer plant project in Sri Lanka, and designing heat exchangers for Lummus UK) to technical service agreements with Iraqi petrochemicals organizations. These agreements, with the Iraqi State Organization for Oil Projects (SOOP) and the State Organization for Industrial Design and Construction (SOIDC), are an interesting example of technology transfer from one developing country to another. Under them EIL deputed technical staff to the two organizations and provided specialized training in India for their engineering personnel.[19] The company has also won some important contracts in Algeria, including a Rs. 2 crore subcontract (to Pullman-Kellogg) for project management and progress and cost monitoring for a $1 billion gas liquefaction project, and a technical services contract with the state utility Sonatrach for Rs. 4 crore for design, engineering, procurement, construction supervision, and commissioning of a series of new products pipelines.

Power and Irrigation

The lion's share of WAPCOS' business has been overseas. Out of fees of Rs. 2.08 crore earned in 1977–8, Rs. 1.82 crore came from assignments in Afghanistan, Bhutan, Burma, Cambodia, Indonesia, Iraq, Laos, Malaysia, Mauritius, Nepal, Nigeria, Philippines, Singapore, Sri Lanka, and Tanzania. WAPCOS' services cover feasibility surveys and the design, construction, and supervision of irrigation, drainage, land reclamation, flood control, and water supply projects, with a similar spread of activity in power generation (thermal and hydro), transmission, and distribution. Some of its assignments have been awarded by the FAO and the World Bank.

TCE in 1976–7 provided technical advice, operation management, and personnel training for thermal power stations in Iran, installed a

5 × 50 MW gas turbine station in Kuwait, provided design services for Deutsche Babcock's thermal projects, and undertook the engineering and construction supervision of a 2 × 120 MW thermal station in Malaysia. More recent assignments have included the provision of technical management services to the Liberian Electric Corporation, and the design, engineering, and construction supervision of two supergrid substations in Iraq.

Railways

RITES was set up in 1974 to bring under one organization the various consultancy activities that Indian Railways had previously provided on an *ad hoc* basis. Its assignments have included techno-economic surveys for new lines in Iran and Syria, systems studies of existing lines in Ghana and Iran, and design work for Asian Development Bank projects in the Philippines and Sri Lanka. It has also provided consultancy services for the general improvement of railway systems in Egypt, New Zealand, Saudi Arabia, the Republic of Korea, and Sri Lanka. In 1978 it put in a strong bid for the Rs. 1,500 crore 600 km Baghdad-Hussaiba railway project and seemed confident of winning it, or at any rate a major part of it. The contract was in fact won by Mendoza Junior of Brazil. Indian commentators ascribed the loss of this prestigious project to over-reliance on political influence and failure to link it to long-term purchases of Iraqi crude in part payment. It was certainly a major disappointment. Shortly afterwards, however, RITES won a three-year Rs. 20 crore contract to manage Nigeria's entire railway system, and it was bidding for further major projects in Iraq.

Industrial Planning

The NIDC has provided consultancy services on various aspects of industrial planning in Guyana, Kuwait, Libya, Tanzania, and a number of other developing countries, ranging from planning industrial estates (Guyana, Kuwait, and Tanzania), establishing national consultancy services (Iran and Tanzania), upgrading existing industries (Tanzania), and setting up technical documentation centres (Guyana, Iran, and Tanzania) to preparing complete national industrial development plans (perspective plan for Iranian capital goods industry and the five-year Libyan industrial development plan for 1976–80). Closely linked with some of this general industrial development work has been the preparation of feasibility studies and the establishment of machine tool plants in Kuwait and Iraq (in association with the CMTI and HMT respectively). HMT has also on its own account provided consultancy services, such as the preparation in 1978 of a project report for a machine tool plant in Iraq.

Other Areas

The foregoing paragraphs may give the impression that in their export work Indian consultants rarely operate outside the fields just discussed. That would in fact be far from the truth. The discussion was presented in this way in an attempt to arrange consultants' activities so as to mirror those of their compatriots in contracting. To give a completely rounded account would be beyond the scope of this book, but of course Indian consultancy firms have won numerous contracts in a number of other fields, such as paper recycling and manufacture (feasibility studies by NIDC in Guyana and Kenya respectively); fish processing (planning study by NIDC, Maldives); glass manufacture (planning study by NIDC, Sri Lanka); management (particularly by TCS); textile mills (feasibility studies and plans by Birla Consultants, Sudan); cement works (engineering and procurement for 2 × 1,600 tpd plants in Iraq by Development Consultants Pvt. and technical services for a cement plant in Syria by Bridge & Roof); and building and town planning (housing and town planning throughout the Gulf by CES and Misurata steel township in Libya by Charles Correa). Although this account is already well-nigh indigestible many further examples could be given and I hope these last few paragraphs will serve to illustrate the diversity and recent achievements of Indian consultancy services overseas, and through them the extent to which India has become a transferrer of technology to other developing countries.

Notes

[1] Details of the contracts described in this chapter have been drawn from a number of sources, notably the *Economic Times, Middle Eastern Economic Digest, Economic and Commercial News*, the firms themselves, and diplomatic commercial officers, both Indian and British. All have been at least double checked. Values are mostly quoted in crores of rupees. Some, unfortunately, were obtainable only in terms of US dollars. I have not converted these as the exchange rate has fluctuated throughout the period under study, and most of the contracts have run over more than one year. The average IMF trade conversion factors/market rates (rupees per US dollar) have been as follows:

1971/2	7.444	1975/6	8.653
1972/3	7.706	1976/7	8.939
1973/4	7.791	1977/8	8.563
1974/5	7.976	1978/9 (Apr.-Dec.)	8.211

As a very rough rule of thumb (good enough to suggest an idea of order of magnitude for the purposes of this chapter), one can regard a crore (10 million) of rupees as approximately 1.25 million US dollars.

[2] In Oct. 1978 the Indian government relaxed the rules so as to permit cash remittances to purchase equity in trading and consultancy services abroad.

[3] Lecraw found that transnational companies originating from other developing countries offered significant benefits to the Thai economy without many of the costs associated with other foreign direct investments. One of the factors influencing a decision to invest was the need to increase the chances of survival of their firm by operating in as many countries as possible, thus spreading their risks. Often their existing associates in Thailand were of the same race (and India provided the highest number of examples in the sample) or even relatives of the principals of the investing LDC transnational company. D. Lecraw, 'Direct Investment by Firms from Less-Developed Countries', *Oxford Economic Papers,* 29/3 (1977).

[4] The increasing attention being paid by Indian investors to the Middle East can be seen by comparing numbers and value of joint ventures already in production in mid-1979 with those under implementation. The Middle East accounted for only 2.5 per cent of the former, but 10.7 per cent of the latter. Southeast Asia, however, remained the clear favourite, with 58 per cent and 54.8 per cent respectively.

Region	In production			Under implementation		
	No. of units	Actual Indian equity (Rs. mn)	Percentage	No. of units	Approved Indian equity (Rs. mn)	Percentage
Southeast Asia	50	160.6	58.0	33	230.2	54.8
South Asia	5	3.0	1.1	9	45.7	10.9
Middle East	15	7.1	2.5	23	44.8	10.7
Africa	23	99.9	36.1	16	83.1	19.7
Europe and America	14	6.4	2.3	8	16.3	3.9
Totals	107	277.0	100.0	89	420.1	100.0

Source: Adapted from *Economic and Commercial News,* 16 June 1979, p. 5.

[5] *Financial Times,* 14 Aug. 1978.

[6] In a performance certificate dated 8 Mar. 1979, issued to mark the completion of the first unit.

[7] *Economic Times,* 29 Sept. 1978. In a follow-up report, dated 6 Oct. 1978, the *Economic Times* maintained that EPI had managed to win the Ardiya project only by submitting a tender 60 per cent lower than that of its nearest

competitor and that the project had been a 'non-starter' from the very beginning. (Certainly in Apr. 1979 EPI officials on the site told me that the company did not expect to make a profit.) According to the same report EPI resorted to similar tactics in order to win its Kuwaiti army camp project in the autumn of 1978, by cutting its original Rs. 105 crore tender down to Rs. 75 crore, prompting the Industrial Development Bank of India (which arranged the export credit) to 'express surprise'. Meanwhile a group of Janata MPs had written to the Prime Minister to 'express their concern over the working conditions in Kuwait' and to demand that EPI be investigated by a parliamentary committee.

A different complexion was put on the Ardiya labour problems by one of EPI's local associates, which alleged that most of them had been 'engineered by the agents of the multinationals', who were piqued at not winning the contract.

By Apr. 1979 all these recriminations had fizzled out and the project, according to the Kuwait National Housing Authority, was progressing smoothly. It certainly looked very impressive. And the labour camp looked much like most other labour camps in the Gulf: airconditioned portable aluminium buildings used as dormitories, with communal messing.

[8] EPI's complete list of overseas projects under implementation in March 1979 was as follows:

Project	Client	Location	Value (US$ mn)
INDUSTRIAL			
Central Grain Silos, Iraq	State Organization for Buildings (SOB) and State Grain Organization, Iraq	Khanakin, Baquba, Tuz	51.21
Northern Grain Silos, Iraq	SOB and State Grain Organization, Iraq	Sinjar, Shirkat, Talafar	56.09
Water treatment plant, Thailand	Metropolitan Water Works Authority, Bangkok	Bangkok	1.50
CIVIL AND STRUCTURAL WORKS			
Ruwais Refinery, Abu Dhabi	Abu Dhabi National Oil Co., Abu Dhabi	Abu Dhabi	24.39
Radio & Colour TV Centre expansion, Iraq	Mitsubishi Corporation, Tokyo, for Ministry of Information, Iraq	Baghdad	16.46
Water Research Centre, Iraq	Ministry of Irrigation, Iraq	Baghdad	18.90
SAAD-3, military infrastructure, Iraq	State Organization for Technical Industries, Iraq	Yarmouk	51.21
35th Brigade camp, Kuwait	Ministry of Defence, Kuwait	Kuwait	97.68

Table in n.8—*cont'd*

Project	Client	Location	Value (US$ mn)
Sief Palace extension, Kuwait	Ministry of Public Works, Kuwait	Kuwait	39.80
Housing Project at Ardiya, Kuwait	National Housing Authority, Kuwait	Kuwait	280.40
Wadi Jizan electrification scheme, Saudi Arabia	Bharat Heavy Electricals Ltd for Electricity Corporation, Saudi Arabia	Jizan	22.46
Aviation fuel storage tanks, Saudi Arabia	Petrola, Athens	Jeddah	6.20

Note: There are discrepancies between the values quoted above by EPI and those shown in Appendices 20, 21, and 24. They may be occasioned by constantly varying rates of exchange and/or by revisions or varying definitions of the contracts involved.

[9] This project was situated close to the Ugandan border and implementation was held up by the border conflict between the two states.

[10] *Financial Times*, 26 Sept. 1977.

[11] The most powerful non-ministerial committee in the Indian government structure, composed of the permanent heads ('Secretaries') of government departments.

[12] Partly, it seems, owing to two unfortunate errors in the tender documents for the civil works subcontract. BHEL was reported to have let the subcontract to GIL on the basis of an estimated 25,000 m³ of earth moving and 424 tonnes of structural steel, whereas the real requirements turned out to be 125,000 m³ and 2,400 tonnes respectively. As a result BHEL apparently had to pay GIL an extra Rs. 23 crore, thus ensuring a loss on the project as a whole (*Economic Times*, 28 Apr. 1979).

[13] This, despite its Saudi location, is a not altogether inappropriate designation. The Wadi Jizan is comparatively fertile, since, like the Yemen with which it marches, it benefits slightly from the wet monsoon winds of the Arabian Sea. It is also partially irrigated. Nevertheless there is still plenty of sand, quite enough to make life very uncomfortable when the midday wind blows.

[14] The Malaysian authorities seem to have had full confidence in BHEL's boilers (built under collaboration with Combustion Engineering of USA). But in order to gain Malaysian acceptance of the associated 120 MW turbogenerator in the first of these Malaysian orders, BHEL had to absorb a 30 per cent price loading so that its tender of a little over $50 million became notionally nearly $67 million for comparison with other offers. This 30 per cent was thus the Malaysians' measure of the inferiority of BHEL's turboset technology (Prem Shankar Jha, *Economic Times*, 11 May 1979).

[15] For instance, a turnkey contract for two substations in Algeria by Tata Exports Ltd for Rs. 3.1 crore, the process control instrumentation for a power station in Malaysia by Instrumentation Ltd for Rs. 3.3 crore, and a substation for the Japanese aid programme in Nepal by Crompton Greaves for Rs. 1.8 crore.

[16] Association of Indian Engineering Industry, *Handbook of Statistics 1978*.

[17] Algeria, Austria, Bangladesh, Brazil, Colombia, Cyprus, Egypt, FRG, GDR, Indonesia, Iran, Cambodia, Laos, Libya, Madagascar, Mauritius, Morocco, Nepal, Sri Lanka, Syria, Thailand, UAE, Venezuela, Vietnam, Yugoslavia, and Zambia.

[18] The Industrial Development Centre for Arab States, UNIDO, and the World Bank.

[19] *SOOP projects.* EIL has provided technical assistance for design, engineering, and project management services to SOOP for the execution of the following pipeline projects: (a) Nassiriya-Kut multi-product pipeline —diameter 8 in, length 185 km; (b) heated fuel oil pipeline from Basrah refinery to Hartha power station—diameter 12 in, length 30 km; (c) branch crude oil pipeline from Buzurgan to Hartha power station—diameter 10 in, length 4.5 km; (d) Nassiriya crude oil pipeline—diameter 12 in, length 27 km; (e) Nassiriya gas pipeline—diameter 14 in, length 175 km; (f) Haditha-Rumaila crude oil pipeline; (g) Iraq-Turkey crude oil pipeline. SOOP also awarded a contract to EIL for tender preparation for the Muftiah jetty project.

SOIDC projects. (a) A team of EIL process engineers assisted SOIDC engineers in the design review and in the review of detailed engineering and construction drawings/documents of the petrochemical complex No. 1 being put up at Basrah by Lummus, USA, for SOIDC; (b) at the request of SOIDC, EIL sent a team in March 1976 to evaluate the naphtha cracker proposal made by Toyo Engineering, Japan, for the petrochemical complex No. 2; (c) EIL engineers helped SOIDC supervise the construction of its Khor-al-Zubair fertilizer plant, which was being put up by Mitsubishi Heavy Industries.

4

Export Promotion and Credit

RESPONSIBILITY for all foreign trade rests with the Ministry of Commerce. In practice the Ministry concentrates on policy and licensing. Responsibility for export promotion, financing, and guarantees is devolved. But the Ministry is represented on the various inter-agency committees concerned with exports and indeed chairs many of them. Actual physical exporting is undertaken by commodity boards (in the case of tea, coffee, cardamom, rubber, coir, and silk); by the State Trading Corporation (STC) and its various offshoots such as the Projects and Equipment Corporation (PEC), Handicraft and Handloom Export Corporation (HHEC), and the Chemicals and Pharmaceuticals Corporation (CPC); by certain other 'canalizing' agencies such as the Minerals and Metals Trading Corporation (MMTC), and by licensed 'export houses' which may be either actual manufacturers or agents acting for manufacturers.

Promotion

Promotion is primarily in the hands of the relevant export promotion council or commodity board. These councils and boards are government funded. The relevant exporters or sectors are of course represented on them. In the case of engineering goods, with which we are principally concerned here, promotion is masterminded by the Engineering Export Promotion Council (EEPC). The EEPC is based in Calcutta, with subsidiary offices in Delhi, Bombay, and Madras, and overseas offices in half a dozen countries including the UAE (Dubai) and the UK.[1] Besides undertaking the normal range of promotional activities the EEPC is an invaluable source of statistics and publishes the very comprehensive annual *Handbook of Export Statistics*.

The engineering industries promote themselves through their own trade association, the Association of Indian Engineering Industry

(AIEI). This is based in Delhi, and it too is a useful source of statistical and other information, which is collated in a statistical handbook published every two or three years.[2] The AIEI is India's apex organization for the promotion of joint venture projects in third countries. In 1979, with this type of collaboration with the UK in mind, it posted a representative to London and located him in the offices of the South Asia Committee in the CBI.

The Federation of Indian Export Organizations (FIEO), based in New Delhi, acts as a co-ordinating body and brings together the various export promotion activities of individual promotion councils, commodity boards, chambers of commerce, and so on. It also helps consultancy organizations to explore the possibilities of overseas contracts.

Export promotion, particularly when it relates to exports through outward Indian investment (normally joint ventures), is undertaken by the Indian Investment Centre (IIC), a body which is otherwise, as its name implies, concerned with selling the attractions of India as a host country for foreign investment. The IIC is based in Delhi and has offices in the capitals of the major industrial countries, including London. It is a useful source of information on Indian technological capabilities.

Small- and medium-scale manufacturers with little or no experience of exporting are encouraged and helped to break into the export market by another government agency, the Trade Development Board.

Physical promotion—that is, participation in and organization of trade fairs and other exhibitions—is the responsibility of the Trade Fair Authority of India, a public sector company under the aegis of the Ministry of Commerce. The Authority publishes a useful weekly promotional journal, *Economic and Commercial News*.

Indian embassies and other diplomatic posts undertake export promotion work in much the same way as their British counterparts. Commercial staff overseas report to the Ministry of Commerce, though they are for the most part members of the Indian Foreign Service (IFS). Use is made of locally engaged staff, often themselves of Indian origin, and staff are also seconded from Commerce and other ministries to posts abroad. Old habits die hard, and it is still possible to detect a feeling among IFS officers, particularly the older ones, that commercial work does not carry quite the same *cachet* as chancery, or political, work. Attitudes are, however changing, and certainly commercial work is given very high priority in Indian missions in the Middle Eastern countries with which this book is mainly concerned.

Export Financing

Export finance is more complicated, as is only to be expected. At the time of writing all the Indian licensed scheduled banks authorized to deal in foreign exchange are involved. In practice this means for the most part the large nationalized banks, but some of the smaller, non-nationalized ones also provide export finance, as of course do the foreign banks. As far as short-term export credit requirements are concerned, the commercial banks operate on their own.[3] But for longer-term requirements recourse is had to the services of the Industrial Development Bank of India (IDBI).

IDBI is the apex development finance institution of India. It provides direct financial assistance to industry, and co-ordinates the activities of all the other industrial development finance institutions at both the all-India and state levels. It also has some of the functions of an export-import bank, acting partly on its own and partly in conjunction with the commercial banks. Its main export services are (i) overseas buyers' credits;[4] (ii) lines of credit to overseas financial institutions;[5] (iii) guarantees (i.e. bid bonds, advance payment guarantees, performance guarantees, etc., *not* export credit guarantees, on which see below); (iv) overseas investment finance; (v) direct financial assistance to exporters;[6] and (vi) export credit refinance.[7]

IDBI participates with the commercial banks in the issue of various kinds of performance guarantees (iii above) and so on to importers overseas on behalf of Indian exporters of engineering goods and services.

Something of a new departure is marked by (iv), outward investment financing. For exchange control reasons Indian promoters of joint ventures in foreign countries had been restricted to investments in kind (i.e. plant and machinery), and IDBI's role had therefore been confined to the financing of these exported hardware investments. But India's increasingly healthy levels of foreign exchange reserves enabled the government in the autumn of 1978 to relax the rules and permit cash remittances for investment in marketing and distributive organizations as well as manufacturing concerns. IDBI's involvement in the exporting of cash for the issue of equity capital in Indian investors' names started in March 1979 and seemed likely to grow fairly rap.dly.

Export Credit Guarantees

India's export credit guarantees apparatus is in the hands of the Export Credit and Guarantee Corporation Ltd (ECGC). This is a public sector corporation and it is not as closely modelled on Britain's

ECGD (which is an independent government department) as its title might imply. Its activities lay greater stress on guaranteeing Indian banks against default by Indian exporters than on guaranteeing exporters against overseas political and commercial risks. Nevertheless its guarantee functions, despite the different emphasis, cover much the same ground as ECGD's, including since September 1978 overseas investment insurance. It does not, however, itself lend money.[8]

Export Incentives

Indian exporters can take advantage of a number of forms of financial incentives, of which the most significant are (i) concessionary rates of interest on export finance; (ii) cash assistance; (iii) duty drawback; (iv) tax incentives; and (v) import replenishment licences.

Interest rate concessions (i above) can amount to as much as 8.5 per cent and even the shortest-term preshipment loan generally attracts a discount of 2.5—4 per cent when measured against ordinary commercial rates for bank advances. In February 1979, for instance, the commercial rate lay between 13.5 per cent and 15 per cent. Preshipment loans were at 11 per cent for up to 90 days (180 days for engineering goods) and 13 per cent for 91–135 days (181–270 days for engineering goods). Postshipment credits were at 11 per cent for a maximum of 90 days. Medium-term export credits provided by banks and fully refinanced by IDBI were 8 per cent with refinance at 6.5 per cent, and IDBI's direct assistance scheme worked out, after allowance was made for the participating banks' rate, at 7.5 per cent.

Cash assistance (ii above) is provided by the government to exporters of mainly non-traditional goods. The main purpose is said to be to enable exporters to penetrate new markets and establish a sustained demand for their products. Government officials sometimes also maintain that it is nothing more than a form of compensation for various kinds of internal taxes (mainly state sales tax and inter-state octroi duties[9]) for which no duty drawback is otherwise available. Its rates, and the range of goods for which it is available, change frequently and apparently fairly arbitrarily. Engineering goods have consistently attracted the highest rates; in February 1979 they ranged between 10 and 20 per cent, depending on product, and over the years 1970/1 to 1974/5 they averaged about 14.5 per cent. Examples of other rates in February 1979 were: textiles 7.5–12.5 per cent; steel 10.5 per cent; processed food 15 per cent; and fresh fruit 10 per cent.

One might expect that, if the true reason for cash assistance was simply to enable mainly non-traditional exports to penetrate new markets, the rates and amounts paid would remain roughly static and even drop occasionally. Instead the general trend was upward, fairly gently in the case of rates and fairly steeply in the case of the cost to the Indian exchequer as more products became eligible and exports have increased. Totals for the years 1974/5–1977/8 were as follows:

> 1974/5 Rs. 66.8 crore (engineering goods Rs. 31.63 crore);
> 1975/6 Rs. 136.0 crore (engineering goods Rs. 58.15 crore);
> 1976/7 Rs. 226.6 crore (engineering goods Rs. 70.33 crore);
> 1977/8 Rs. 311.0 crore (engineering goods Rs. 102.19 crore).

The total for 1978/9 was expected to be about Rs. 400 crore.[10]

The totals for engineering goods quoted above give rates (totals/ FOB exports) of 9.1 per cent, 14.2 per cent, 12.7 per cent, and 16.3 per cent for the four years quoted, a wide enough spread to cast doubt on the official thesis that cash assistance is simply a rebate for sales tax and octroi duty, the unit cost of neither of which to engineering exporters is likely to have varied nearly so much. One is forced to conclude that cash assistance is at best a regulator (though one with a fairly stiff upward ratchet) and at worst an acknowledgement that Indian engineering goods were overpriced (or perhaps that the rupee was overvalued).[11] One thing seem fairly certain: cash assistance for engineering exports had come to stay.[12]

Duty drawback (iii above) is available in order to offset excise duties and customs duties paid by exporters on respectively domestic and imported materials used in the manufacture of their goods. As with cash assistance, the rates payable are revised from time to time and are usually calculated on an industry-wide basis rather than case by case. For obvious reasons manufactured exports attract the lion's share, and, since India traditionally charges very high rates of customs duties on components and other inputs, a duty drawback system is unavoidable if manufactured exports are to be competitive, as must be the case with any exporting country protected by high tariffs. The government recognized the importance of the principle of duty-free inputs to such an extent that in 1978 it introduced a procedure whereby an exporter can obtain immediate payment against the duty drawback entitlement from his banker by way of an interest-free advance immediately after the shipment has been effected. This system also of course helps offset the effects of inflation on the true value of the drawback.

Tax incentives (iv above) amount as far as direct taxation is concerned to no more than allowance against the income tax liability of expenses incurred in market development and export promotion.[13] On indirect taxation—besides the duty drawback scheme described above—export sales do not attract central sales tax (as distinct from state sales tax, which, as explained above, is theoretically offset by cash assistance).

Under the complex system of licensing by which Indian industry is regulated exporters are entitled to a privileged share of import replenishment licences (v above). These have a value not only because they are to a certain extent transferable but also because they are for the purchase of imports with free foreign exchange (as distinct from licences tied, for instance, to bilateral aid and therefore to procurement from a particular country) and because the inputs purchasable with them have a scarcity value. However, the value of replenishment licences, and therefore their effectiveness as an export incentive, must decline so long as the current trend towards import liberalization, with more and more goods switched to open general licences, continues.

There are of course other forms of export incentives, such as for instance freight subsidies and steel price differentials, but the five briefly discussed above are those of greatest consequence.

Possibilities for Reorganization

The picture that emerges of the whole infrastructure of exporting from India is one of considerable complexity, not to say confusion. And yet the *ad hoc* nature of the apparatus is understandable. Institutions were created or adapted as new circumstances arose, as indeed the role of India was transformed—rapidly transformed—from that of an exporter of agricultural produce and simple manufactures (mainly textiles) to that of a country transferring technology to other LDCs in an increasingly sophisticated range of products and services. That there was no clean sweep of institutions merely reflects the wide diversity of interests at work in a democratically governed mixed economy.

Calls for reorganization are of course made, particularly in financing, which many Indian officials believe could be better performed by a single Exim Bank.[14] They argue that the establishment of an Exim Bank should not only result in more streamlined (and less time-consuming and therefore cheaper) procedures, but also that a single major institution would dispose of funds on the sort of scale that will be needed if Indian firms are to be able to continue competing for overseas projects, which tend to grow ever larger.[15] Indeed there is a tendency on the part of exporters and promotional bodies such as the EEPC to complain that Indian export credit is both too short and too scarce to enable them to compete on equal terms. IDBI disputes this view, claiming that no worthwhile export project ever suffers from a shortage of export finance.

IDBI's role in the gradual build-up of export financing is instructive. At first it was one merely of refinancing. But in 1968, to help meet the demands consequent on a rapidly developing switch from low to high value goods for export, IDBI introduced its direct participation scheme whereby it entered the risk arena, the effect of its intervention being to reduce the overall rate of postshipment finance by 0.5 per cent. Within a few years the scheme had been extended to cover turnkey projects as well as supply contracts, and the buyers' credits and lines of credit described above had been added to the Bank's services, the latter being for the benefit mainly of exports to other non-oil developing countries. In June 1975 financing procedures were simplified to the extent that IDBI became the focal point for the export finance bureaucracy. In 1979 it chaired the working group which gives final clearance to proposals for export finance, the other institutions represented being the Reserve Bank, the commercial bank concerned, ECGC, the Ministry of Finance, and the appropriate functional ministry.[16] Indeed IDBI had already laid the foundations for an Exim Bank.

Notes

[1] The others are Kenya Philippines, Singapore, USA, and West Germany.

[2] One was published in Jan. 1979.

[3] The banks provide preshipment and postshipment finance. The former, commonly referred to in India as a 'packing credit', is extended to exporters against confirmed orders or letters of credit. Any advance has to be repaid from the proceeds of the relevant export bills. In Mar. 1979 maximum rates of interest were 11 per cent per annum. As an incentive to banks providing finance at concessional rates to exporters, the Reserve Bank pays a subsidy at the rate of 1.5 per cent. The terms for packing credit are 90 days from the date of advance except for specified medium and heavy engineering goods and construction contracts for which they may extend to 180 days. Advances are normally based on the FOB value of the order.

Postshipment credits are available from the date of the extension of the credit, after shipment of the goods, to the date of realization of export proceeds. Under Indian exchange control regulations payments against exports must normally be received in India within 180 days of the date of shipment.

⁴ Under the overseas buyers' credit scheme IDBI grants credits to foreign buyers for the import of capital goods from India. The exporter's obligation is to fulfil the commercial terms of the export contract; once this is done he is paid out of the credit on a non-recourse basis. IDBI's share does not normally exceed 50 per cent, with the balance coming from the commercial banks, though in longer-term cases (i.e. over 7 years) IDBI may pass on to the participating banks a larger than pro-rata share of the earlier maturities. These credits have no maximum limit and are rarely granted for amounts of less than Rs. 1 crore. The currency of repayment is usually but not necessarily rupees. The period of repayment is fixed according to the nature of the project, the value of the contract, the estimated value of the outflow of foreign exchange, etc. The interest generally works out at 7.5 per cent net of the cost of guarantees, stamp duty, etc. A commitment fee of 0.5 per cent is usually payable on the undisbursed balance of the credit sanctioned by IDBI. The security is normally in the form of an acceptable bank guarantee, bills accepted by a bank, or promissory notes executed by government buyers.

⁵ IDBI grants lines of credit to overseas financial institutions to enable them to finance borrowers in their respective countries who wish to import machinery and capital equipment from India, thus saving the importer the need to negotiate terms individually with Indian suppliers or financial institutions. The borrowing (overseas) institutions can quote their own terms to the end users. The procedures and means of operation of this scheme are, *mutatis mutandis*, the same as those of the overseas buyers' credit scheme.

⁶ Under this scheme the exporter obtains credit either from IDBI alone or from IDBI and one or more commercial banks. The term loans involved are intended to finance the export of engineering goods and services on deferred payment terms. While the object of the scheme is to match foreign credit terms, the maximum periods of the loans are restricted (3 years for loans of up to Rs. 1 million, 5 years for loans between Rs. 1 million and Rs. 5 million, 7 years for loans between Rs. 5 million and Rs. 1 crore, and 10 years for those over Rs. 1 crore) and in any case are not normally extended beyond the life span of the project concerned. Special, and generally more liberal, terms are negotiated individually for turnkey projects.

⁷ The object of the scheme is to encourage commercial banks to provide term export credits to Indian exporters. Eligible banks (i.e. licensed scheduled banks authorized to deal in foreign exchange in India) can avail themselves of the facility to the full extent of the term loans granted by them to exporters. The scheme provides for refinance against postshipment credits granted by eligible banks for periods between 6 months and 15 years to exporters—who must be manufacturers, recognized export houses, or other exporters of standing, and is intended for the execution of overseas projects in which the bulk of the equipment, materials, and services is exported from India on deferred terms.

⁸ The ECGC provides the following forms of cover: (i) *Packing Credit Guarantee*. Covers risks of loss to the bank due to the insolvency or protracted default of the exporter in respect of Packing Credit advances. Losses to the

extent of 66.66 per cent of the amount of loss, subject to a maximum liability fixed under the guarantee, are paid by the Corporation. (ii) *Postshipment Export Credit Guarantee.* Covers advances granted at postshipment stage for the purpose of purchase, discount, or negotiation of export bills. Risks covered: insolvency or protracted default to repay debt. The Corporation bears 75 per cent of a loss. (iii) *Export Finance Guarantee.* Covers advances to exporters at postshipment stage against export benefits (i.e. cash assistance, duty drawback, etc.) receivable from the government. Risks covered: insolvency or protracted default of the exporter. The Corporation bears 75 per cent of a loss. (iv) *Export Production Finance Guarantee.* The purpose of this guarantee is to enable banks to sanction advances to the extent of 50 per cent over and above the FOB value of the shipment subject to a limit of 100 per cent of the domestic value of the export product. Advances may be sanctioned at preshipment or postshipment stage. Risks up to 66.66 per cent of any loss incurred due to the insolvency of the exporter or his protracted default are covered. (v) *Export Performance Guarantee.* This guarantee has been evolved to help exporters to secure, on easier terms, bank guarantees they have to furnish in the export business, i.e. either without making a cash deposit or against a reduced margin. It covers risk up to 66.66 per cent of a loss sustained by the bank as the result of the insolvency or protracted default of the exporter.

In addition ECGC offers: (vi) *Whole turnover postshipment export credit guarantee,* which covers the whole turnover of the bank. (vii) *Comprehensive risks policy* covering commercial and political risks. (viii) *Special Scheme for Small-Scale Exporters.*

[9] A duty levied on goods crossing state borders.

[10] *Economic Times,* 13 Mar. 1979.

[11] Most Indian officials would discount this possibility. They would argue that fluctuations in currency values do not apply in an economy, such as India's, in which imports and exports are controlled administratively and the currency is not convertible. Also it must be conceded that the absence of a significant foreign exchange black market, at any rate during the early months of 1979, would suggest that the rupee rate was reasonably realistic then.

[12] Informal official opinion in Delhi in Mar. 1979 was that this was indeed likely. India could and would continue to afford a fairly generous measure of cash assistance since it was not a true cost to the economy, being (at least in theory) merely a reimbursement of otherwise non-refundable taxes.

[13] A concession allowed under Section 35B of the 1961 Income Tax Act.

[14] Engineering Export Promotion Council, *Project Exports: Report of the Committee set up to Examine the Recommendations of the Workshop on Project Exports Organized by the Engineering Export Promotion Council at Vigyan Bhavan, New Delhi, on 28 and 29 March 1978* (1978), p. 48.

[15] Ibid., p. 47.

[16] The working group cleared about 5,000 proposals in 1977/8, one in five of which would, on average, be expected to materialize.

5

Migrant Labour

INDIA's most successful export to the Middle East, in cash terms, is labour. Large numbers of Indians, at all levels of skill, migrated[1] to the Middle East during the 1970s and most of them have been remitting home a very considerable proportion of their earnings.

Remittances

The precise value of this export trade in people, or the work that they do, is the subject of considerable mystery and disagreement. The main problem is that India's invisible receipts have grown so rapidly that the published statistics, at the time of writing, have not caught up with them. The World Bank estimated, in time for the June 1979 meeting of the India aid consortium, that net invisible receipts were running at $2 billion in 1977/8 and 1978/9, of which current transfers accounted for $1.3 billion to $1.4 billion. This massive inflow was more than enough to cover the trade deficit, provisionally estimated for 1978/9 at Rs. 1,062 crore,[2] or $1.3 billion, and comfortably exceeded India's net receipts of foreign aid, estimated for the same year at $743 million.[3] According to the Reserve Bank of India,[4] inward remittances for the years 1974/5 to 1977/8 were as follows:

1974/5	Rs. 654 crore	1976/7	Rs. 1,586 crore
1975/6	Rs. 1,198 crore	1977/8	Rs. 2,117 crore

In dollar terms this would mean an inflow of about $2.5 billion in 1977/8, even higher than the World Bank's estimate. Others put it as high as Rs. 200 crore a month.[5] The current Five Year Plan, however, is counting on an annual average of only Rs. 400 crore[6] over the period 1978/83.[7]

No one really knows precisely where all this money has been coming from. Some presumably comes from countries with a tradition of Indian immigration such as the UK, USA, and Canada.

47

But in view of its rapid growth since the 1973/4 oil crisis, and on the assumption that transfers from the roughly static number of people permanently settled in the UK, USA, and Canada would themselves tend to remain static or slowly decline, it is a fairly safe bet that much if not most of it was coming from the Middle East, where most Indian workers have no intention of settling permanently, having gone there on a deliberately short- or medium-term earning spree. This is certainly the view of most recent commentators and borne out by observation on the spot in the Gulf.

A Tradition

There is nothing very new about Indians seeking their fortune overseas. The British empire permitted free movement between and settlement (within limits) in imperial territories. But far the most significant factor in Indian migration during imperial times was the system of indentured labour,[8] under which large numbers of Indians were moved to distant colonies to provide labour for the new plantation industries that were being established: sugar in Mauritius, Fiji, and Trinidad, and rubber in Malaya. And, on a closer parallel with the conditions of our own time, major civil engineering projects in a labour-deficit area (railway building in East Africa) set off a migration the eventual consequences of which are still being felt in the unhappy saga of the East African Asians.

Migration out of the subcontinent declined to a mere trickle at the outbreak of the First World War[9] and remained so until some fifteen or twenty years after Independence when it started again, but on a different basis and in new directions.[10] This time it consisted, as far as India was concerned (there were of course parallel waves from Pakistan and later Bangladesh) of semi-skilled and skilled Gujaratis and Punjabis looking for employment in the United Kingdom, in many cases exchanging tenuous links with textile mills in Ahmedabad and Ludhiana with better prospects in the mills of Leeds and Bradford and the engineering industries of the West Midlands and outer London. At the same time there was a steady but far smaller flow of people with marketable professional skills (mainly medical and engineering) to the United Kingdom, Canada, and the United States. Like their earlier predecessors in British imperial possessions, these new overseas Indian communities maintained strong links with 'home', even though settlement was almost always on a permanent basis, with regular remittances of money to relatives in India becoming an established pattern. As in the case of the earlier migrations, political changes resulted in due course in the closure (or at any rate severe restriction) of these avenues of exodus.

Meanwhile a new pattern had begun to develop, with the employment of growing numbers of Indians in the oil-producing countries of the Persian Gulf, mainly as traders, professionals, and domestics. The construction boom that followed the major increase in these countries' purchasing power in 1973–4 greatly increased their demand for labour, particularly skilled and semi-skilled, which India was well placed geographically and socially to help fill. And when Indian construction firms began to win contracts there they naturally took their own labour forces with them. Indeed their ability to provide large numbers of comparatively low-paid men with all the necessary skills must have been a significant factor in their ability to win contracts.

Numbers

It is not known exactly how many Indians have migrated to the worksites of the Gulf. Indian embassies and foreign diplomats in the countries concerned in 1979 suggested the following:[11]

Bahrain:	13,000	Qatar:	25,000
Kuwait:	70,000	Saudi Arabia:	80,000– 90,000
Oman:	50,000–60,000	UAE:	150,000–200,000

Or perhaps a total of between 400,000 and 500,000. They based these figures partly on the passport and visa returns, on other contacts made in the course of routine consular work, and partly on guesswork. They admitted that they were likely to have firm information only about those migrants who had entered legally, with a passport and visa, or who had entered illegally and subsequently sought to legitimize their presence. Illegal Indian immigrants were thought to be present in particularly large numbers in the UAE, to which there was a well-patronized undercover service by motorboat from the Indian west coast, and Saudi Arabia, where considerable numbers of Haj pilgrims were thought to 'disappear' in search of employment.

According to the Reserve Bank of India,[12] emigration of Indians (to all destinations) was rising sharply in the period 1975 to 1978 (30,406 in 1975/6, 72,491 in 1976/7 and 86,505 in the nine months ending March 1978), but these figures, despite their unrounded air of authenticity, suffer from the same disadvantage as Indian embassy estimates in that they are based only on numbers of intending travellers who made orthodox and 'legal' financial arrangements before their departure, and must therefore be regarded simply as a useful minimum indication of departing workers.

Passport issues can provide another clue. The Regional Passport Office at Cochin (in Kerala) issued 49,587, 107,846 and 200,997 passports in 1975, 1976, and 1977 respectively,[13] and in 1978 was issuing them at a rate of 32,000 a month, nearly all with one of the Gulf countries as the principal destination.[14] The Indian passport authorities apparently work on the rule of thumb that one in every five passport holders actually leaves the country each year. That may apply (or may have applied) on an all-India basis, but it is difficult to believe that only one in five of those who successfully completed the bureaucratic obstacle course involved in the acquisition of an Indian passport, who lived in Kerala (the main catchment area) and who stated on their application forms that they intended to visit the Gulf, had any serious intention of going there. A one-in-two rate would mean that going on for 200,000 Keralans went during 1978 in search of employment in the Gulf. These people were all armed with passports; there were many there already of whom there was little if any official cognizance. Indian passports are valid for five years, which means that double-counting on a passport-issue basis had not in 1979 begun to apply in the case of the Gulf, where migration did not start on any significant scale until the oil boom was well under way. Workers recruited for specific projects were normally taken for a year initially, and annual home leave (sometimes paid for by the firm concerned) had become fairly normal practice for 'legal' workers (i.e. the kind with passports who would figure in immigration statistics). But it will be some years yet before official statistics catch up with reality, by which time the Gulf phenomenon may be waning anyway. All in all, 500,000, when one bears in mind that 1978/9 was a peak year, seems a plausible figure for 1979.

Where the Migrants Come From

Indian workers in the Gulf come from all the western half of India, particularly the migrant catchment areas of Punjab, Gujarat, Rajasthan, and Kerala. The lure of well-paid employment has also reached into areas not previously associated with emigration such as Madhya Pradesh, in the capital of which (Bhopal) a new regional passport office was opened in October 1978 to help reduce the pressure in Delhi and Bombay. Sikhs and other Punjabis are very much in evidence in the Gulf, but not to the same extent as in the United Kingdom, possibly because of the growing prosperity of Punjabi agriculture. Indeed most of the Sikhs in the Gulf are said to come from places outside the Punjab, particularly Delhi.

There is fairly general agreement that Kerala is the principal source of the migrants. The Keralan State Bureau of Economics and Statistics estimated that there were 135,000 Keralans working abroad (not solely in the Gulf) in 1978, but there are good reasons to believe this to be a serious underestimate.[15] At the other end of the scale figures of 2 million[16] or even 3 million[17] have been seriously suggested, clearly gross overestimates. Nevertheless, so great was the traffic between Kerala and the Gulf that the Indian authorities had in 1978 to upgrade the formerly sleepy provincial airport at Trivandrum to full international status, the only one not serving one of the four 'metropolitan' cities.

There is a long tradition of emigration from Kerala, both within India and abroad.[18] Before Independence those Keralans (speakers of Malayalam, hence frequently referred to as Malayalees) who left India altogether migrated mainly to the British colonies in Southeast Asia, and their descendants are present in large numbers in Burma, Singapore, Sri Lanka, and Borneo. This earlier movement was gradual and spread over many decades. As we have seen, the latest phase, to the Gulf, has been much more sudden, and since the oil crisis has assumed some of the characteristics of a gold rush.

The reasons for the exodus of Keralans are demographic, social, and economic. Kerala has only 1.2 per cent of the total land area of India, but it accounts for 4 per cent of its population, and its population density is one of the highest in the world. Arab cultural contact with the west coast of India, especially Kerala, is well established as a result of centuries of sea-borne trade. Persian chieftains (and proselytizers) once held sway in parts of what is now Kerala, and partly as a result of that 20 per cent of the population is Muslim. India's only indigenous Jews have for centuries been centred on Cochin, and Kerala has the largest concentrations of Christians, both Syrian and Catholic, in the country. All these minority religions have of course meant that many Keralans had links with other cultures outside India; the Muslims, many of whom live on the coast, can even speak Arabic. These are some of the factors that have combined to make Keralan society more syncretic and cosmopolitan in outlook than that of any other part of India,[19] with the exceptions perhaps of the major ports and special cases like Goa and Pondicherry.

Kerala has India's highest literacy rate (70 per cent in the 1971 census) and by 1978 was turning out more than 200,000 new matriculates a year.[20] It is also well to the fore in the unemployment stakes, beaten only by Goa (an area with very similar socio-economic characteristics) on a male and remale basis, but with a clear lead on a males-only basis.[21] More particularly, Kerala has by far the highest number of educated unemployed[22] and the highest general unemployment rate.[23] A combination of high unemployment and high literacy is a good recipe for political discontent, and it could well be that the employment opportunities of the Gulf have acted as a safety-valve, giving vent to pent-up energies that might otherwise have been expended on activities of a different nature at home. Certainly well-educated and ambitious Malayalees have been looking beyond the confines of their own homeland for a century at least, and perhaps longer. The links that they have kept with home have reinforced the cosmopolitan nature of Keralan society and stoked up the ambitions of fresh generations of potential expatriates.

Why They Migrate

Kerala may provide an extreme example, but unemployment, particularly among the educated, is a country-wide problem of startling dimensions. The Indian workforce is expected to grow by nearly 6 million a year over the years 1978–83, but, assuming a rate of growth of industrial production of 5 per cent, as in 1977/8,[24] the organized sector will absorb only 2.7 million of the 29.5 million new workers over the period of the Sixth Plan. Numbers of unemployed graduate engineers are expected to increase by half and unemployed diploma-level engineers will more than double.[25] Numbers of job applicants registered on the employment exchanges rose from 2.7 million in 1967 to 10.9 million in 1977.[26] In late 1978 unemployment among degree- and diploma-holding mechanical and electrical engineers was 33.6 per cent and 30.6 per cent respectively.[27] Prospects at home were so poor that 50 per cent of engineering graduates in Delhi were reported to be looking for jobs with salaries of no more than Rs. 300 a month—about the going rate for a middle-grade domestic servant (whose pay would in any case be enhanced by free accommodation, clothing, and some food). The same man would have been paid Rs. 3,500, with all found, by BHEL in Saudi Arabia early in 1979.[28] American firms recruiting in India in 1978 were holding out the prospect of $300–$1,500 a month, depending on level of skill (again all found, including paid annual home leave).[29] No wonder the lure of the Gulf is strong.

Most of the Keralan emigrants were unemployed before they left India, and family indebtedness was a powerful incentive, both for the unemployed and for the few who already had jobs.[30] They originated mainly from three *Taluks* (a subdivision of a District in Kerala), and came mainly from minority communities, Muslim, Ezhava,[31] and Christian. The Muslims and Ezhavas were nearly all unemployed and poorly educated (but only 10 per cent were illiterate), but the Christians mostly had jobs and were well educated.[32] Very few caste Hindus such as Brahmins or Nairs[33] migrated.

What Happens to the Money

As is only to be expected, Kerala has received most of the money that Indian workers in the Middle East remit. Again, estimates vary fairly widely. The average remittance per Keralan migrant seems to have been Rs. 11,700[34] in 1978. (In Gujarat it was slightly higher, at Rs. 13,460[35] but there are far fewer Gujarati migrant workers in the Middle East.) If we assume that there were about 300,000 Keralans in the Middle East in 1978 (the 200,000 who went that year, plus another 100,000 who were already there—a cautious estimate), that would mean an inflow of about Rs. 350 crore (nearly a crore a day) in 1978. Rs. 11,700 per migrant, however, refers to all migrants, including those in Canada and the United States, who are mainly professionals earning high salaries. Since they are also mainly permanent settlers, with families to support abroad, that might cancel out any greater theoretical ability to remit to India. The Indian government suggested Rs. 400 crore as the 1978 Keralan total from all sources,[36] but this seems on the low side if the Middle East accounted for Rs. 350 crore. Foreign diplomats in the Gulf put the total of Indian remittances from Bahrain, Kuwait, Oman, Qatar, Saudi Arabia, and the UAE at Rs. 800 crore.[37] If we assume that 75 per cent of the Indian migrants are Keralans,[38] we arrive at a figure of Rs. 600 crore to Kerala alone. This much higher estimate tallies with one derived from banking sources for 1977,[39] when Rs. 550 crore were alleged to have passed through 48,000 non-resident external accounts.[40] Even if we accept the higher estimates, we must remember that there are about 24 million people in Kerala, which may seem an awful lot of people to share Rs. 550 crore. But in Indian terms it is major sum—an extra Rs. 250 for every man, woman, and child in the state (and, as it happens, roughly the equivalent of the state budget).

In fact of course the remittances are not evenly distributed all over the state. Households receiving money from a migrant abroad admitted to an average of Rs. 15,000 a year in 1978. Some households (in 1977) were receiving only Rs. 10,500, while a few, at the other end of the scale, were getting as much as Rs. 24,000 per migrant.[41] Even Rs. 10,500 would seem a princely sum to many of the households concerned.

An inflow of Rs. 500–600 crore a year could transform Kerala's economy if it were productively invested. But all the evidence seems to point to its being spent on private consumption and the settlement of debts. The government of India introduced the Foreign Currency (Non-Resident) Accounts scheme (FCNRA) in November 1975 as a means of attracting the savings of non-resident Indians to India. These accounts are kept in dollars or sterling, and the balance and interest are repatriable in the same designated foreign currency after one to five years. By the end of 1977 a disappointing Rs. 10.7 crore was on deposit in the 14,269 FCNRA accounts in the three Kerala-based banks, or about Rs. 7,500 per account. And ordinary deposits were increasing at a rate of only about Rs. 75 crore a year.[42]

Living standards in those households fortunate enough to have a member working in the Gulf have risen steeply. So has conspicuous consumption. There is a building boom in the state, of houses, cinemas, and private clinics. Large and gaudy desirable residences have sprung up in even the most rural villages, where they stand incongruously cheek-by-jowl with traditional red pantiled and thatched Keralan village houses. More new cars are sold in Kerala than in any other state with the exception of Maharashtra, West Bengal, and Tamil Nadu (each of which contains one of the four 'metropolitan' cities) and Delhi.[43] Some of the money is hoarded in the traditional form of gold jewellery; Keralan jewellers were well to the fore during the series of gold auctions held by the Reserve Bank in 1978. Little of the money seems to have found its way into more productive or developmental channels, with the doubtful exception of the film and magazine publishing industry. House-building, however, spreads its economic benefits quite widely. Ultimately the multiplier effect of the foreign money can be shown to have spread through the primary and secondary sectors, right down to the tertiary sector.[44]

The Kerala government does not appear to have benefited much from the inflow, though presumably indirect taxation must have risen. The government promoted a savings scheme for cumulative deposits in 1977, but this seems not to have been a success. Thought turned towards the establishment of a new non-banking financial agency (possibly a state unit trust) but it is not clear whether its attractions would be any greater than those available through more orthodox channels, or indeed through the Centre's Unit Trust of India. In offering the government advice on how to get its hands on more of the money the Indian press has tended to dwell on the low level of political and social stability in Kerala and lack of suitable infrastructure which combine to deter expatriate Keralans from investing their earnings in new and productive industrial and agricultural enterprises at home.[45]

Social Consequences

Some of the social consequences of the inflow of money have given rise to concern. Since most Keralan returned migrants have expressed their success in terms of bricks and mortar, generally in their home villages rather than in the towns, rural land values have been pushed to heights unheard of only a year earlier. Prices as high as Rs. 15,000[46] a 'cent' (about 48 square yards) were being paid in 1978 in some villages with a high incidence of emigration, from a base only a year or two earlier of Rs. 400 or 500. Keralans (particularly villagers) without access to Gulf money may be priced out of their own traditional areas. Labour rates, reflecting the shortage of skilled men as a result of emigration and profiting from the local building boom, have also risen. Skilled workers (carpenters, masons, etc.) in 1978 expected about Rs. 22 to Rs. 25 a day, whereas the year before they would have been content with Rs. 14, with commensurate rises for unskilled workers.[47] It is doubtful, however, whether people who earn their living from activities less directly connected with Gulf-derived prosperity have increased their earnings much, if at all. While sky-rocketing land values may be of little concern to most of them they must be adversely affected by the reported steep increase in the cost of staples such as fish.[48]

One of the more undesirable effects of the Gulf boom in Kerala has been the rise of a large and prosperous industry of 'agents' of various sorts ranging from straightforward (and necessary) travel agents to touts and tricksters dealing in bogus job recruitment, 'No Objection' certificates[49] of doubtful validity, and various forms of illegal travel, who regularly relieve intending emigrants of Rs. 10,000 or more for their services. 'Investment' in illegal documents and passages is all too often merely a preliminary to further extortion by the Keralan tout's representative in the Gulf, who requires his cut in order not to expose the illegal immigrant to the local authorities. A migrant of this sort is unlikely to be employed by the sort of company that pays his passage home[50] and there are reports of thousands of unfortunate Indians stranded in the Gulf, unable to afford the fare home and forced meanwhile to continue to pay protection money.[51]

The Janata government having eased travel restrictions, illegal methods ought to lose some of their attraction. Further, in an attempt to protect the welfare of Indians abroad the government introduced in 1978 stricter rules for foreign companies wishing to recruit labour from India, requiring them to comply with a 25-point list of pre-conditions drawn up by the Directorate General of Employment and Training.[52] The points include minimum basic rates of pay, three months' notice of redundancy, thirty days' paid leave a year, free medical services, free furnished accommodation, free transport to and from work, and an undertaking by the employed that each employee will remit at least 10 per cent of his earnings to India. These seem eminently sensible requirements and would undoubtedly have done much to improve the Indian workers' lot had they been introduced three or four years earlier, when Gulf demand for labour was at its highest. Lower demand[53] apart, there are other countries in South Asia with an apparently less fastidious concern for their expatriates' welfare, and there could be a danger that foreign companies might turn to them for labour, at least until they introduce similar measures.

If the Indian government were to take its manpower reforms one logical step further and set up (as the Chairman of EPI, India's biggest overseas contractor, once suggested[54]) an overseas manpower corporation on South Korean lines with powers to satisfy foreign companies in search of labour, it could recoup any ground lost as a result of the introduction of the 25-point scheme. It is after all, already well organized, through the Foreign Assignments Section of the Department of Home Affairs, to supply and protect the interests of professional and higher technical manpower. A register is kept of personnel of this calibre, mainly from the public sector. They are seconded overseas for periods of four or five years during which time their jobs at home are reserved for them and they continue to earn promotion, retirement, and social welfare benefits. In Libya for instance, the Libyan government advises the Indian embassy of its needs and the process of selection then takes place in India; in 1978 this resulted in the secondment there of about 2,500 professionals (1,500 medical staff and the rest mainly university lecturers and engineers attached to various Libyan government departments). Nothing so elaborate is needed, nor would it be feasible, for manual workers, but an overseas manpower corporation that relieved foreign companies of the need to recruit or act through recruiting agents in return for guaranteed and fair conditions of service should not be beyond the realms of possibility.

Efforts have also been made at state level to profit from the recruiting trade and to safeguard the interests of the recruits. In January 1978 the Kerala government set up an organization entitled Overseas Development and Employment Promotion Consultants Ltd in an effort to squeeze out the touts and to syphon off a few rupees into the state treasury at the same time. The agency's first nine months were not a success, and its future was in doubt.[55] Nevertheless the Chief Minister of Madhya Pradesh was reported in October 1978 to be considering, at the suggestion of the Minister for

External Affairs, Mr Vajpayee, setting up a corporation along the lines of that in Kerala 'to ensure fool-proof arrangements for those going abroad in search of jobs and to eliminate bogus employment agencies'.[56] There is certainly room for state agencies of this sort, provided they can be effectively organized.

It should be pointed out, however, in fairness to some of the Indian companies concerned, and especially to EPI (which received a major share of the criticism levelled at them by the Lok Sabha and the Indian press), that living conditions for migrant Indian workers in the Gulf are not universally bad. In 1979 at three of the biggest Indian projects in Kuwait, UAE, and Saudi Arabia[57] members of the workforce were living in new, clean, airconditioned temporary buildings. They were not overcrowded, they were well fed, and they were provided with a reasonable modicum of entertainment and sporting facilities. For many of them life in the Gulf must have seemed luxurious by Keralan peasant or artisan standards.[58]

A more general social consequence, with far wider potential implications, for both good and ill, must be the inequalities and social polarization that remittances have engendered, possibly fuelling caste and class tensions. Most of the newly wealthy are Muslims or low-caste Hindus, hitherto beyond the pale of traditional village society and now resented and envied as the owners of the largest and newest houses in the village and the very noticeable possessors of consumer goods far beyond the reach of higher-caste and more traditional stay-at-homes. Some of the most successful of them have become so socially and economically alienated from their home villages that they have drifted to the towns. There is apparently a 'colony' of these people in the state capital, Trivandrum, and they are known locally as 'the Persians'.[59] But there are also signs that, despite the low-caste origins of many of them, they are beginning to be accepted as husbands for higher-caste girls, with an accompanying considerable increase in the dowry rate.[60] Penetration of the higher castes in this way by the economic power of the lower-caste Gulf workers could conceivably in the long run prove to have been one of the most beneficial of the side-effects of the Keralan Gulf migrant worker wave. It is still too early to tell, and it must be borne in mind that the effects will remain localized.

Most of the migrants have been too busy earning money, or spending it, to have much time for other activities. However, there have been signs that some of them have begun to recognize that their economic strength could be expressed in political terms, that they could form a cohesive group with economic muscle power, and, in short, demand their 'rights'. So far these have scarcely been articulated and have consisted of little more than complaints about minor issues

such as duty-free allowances (returning migrants want to be allowed
to import goods to a value of 25 per cent of their annual remittances).
But the migrants have started to organize themselves, as the Indian
Non-Resident Depositors Association, and in December 1978 they
called for their own representation in the Rajya Sabha (the upper
house of the Indian parliament) and the state Assemblies of Kerala
and the Punjab.[61]

Another, seemingly minor, consequence—but one that probably
looms far larger in the morally conservative surroundings of the
Keralan villages where the migrants come from—is the taste they
have evidently acquired for salacious films and literature, a taste to
which the Keralan film and magazine publishing industries have
pandered with considerable advantage. The films[62] and magazines
concerned, meant primarily for distribution in the labour camps in
the Middle East but also available at home, have given rise to a
lively debate on what many commentators regard as the sapping of
the state's morals.[63]

The Future

The future of Indian labour migration to the Gulf is, of course,
bound up with the future of the Middle Eastern boom itself. It will
be argued later in this book that the boom is not so much running
out of steam as changing its nature. The first mad rush to complete
as many infrastructure projects as possible had begun to slow down
by 1978, if not earlier, particularly in the UAE—with the highest
number of Indian labourers.[64] The countries concerned began to
draw breath, budgets in some cases were feeling the strain, and the
time was approaching when most of their immediate infrastructure
needs would have been met. The ensuing switch to residential and
industrial construction will require smaller armies of foreign labour,
but with a higher proportion of skilled men. India's score on degree
and availability of skills is high (probably the highest in this context),
and, provided the Indian government does not pursue over-restrictive
recruitment measures, this should give her an increasing edge over
the competition as the nature of the boom changes and its labour
requirement becomes technically more demanding. But the advantage will be comparative only, since absolute numbers must surely
soon level out and eventually decline.

Even if the numbers of Indians working in the Gulf do not drop
in the next two or three years there are reasons to think that the
level of remittances could soon begin to do so. Inflation in the Gulf
states could eat into migrant workers' savings unless wages keep
pace. We have seen how the Indian government is counting on a

total receipt over the whole Sixth Plan period of only Rs. 2,000 crore, or Rs. 400 crore a year. Lack of investment opportunities, reduction in interest rates on bank deposits in non-resident accounts, and diversion of remittances into unofficial channels owing to uncertainty over the value of the rupee could together result in a rapid slowing down in the growth of remittances, and possible even in their reduction.[65]

No one knows how many unofficial or illegal Indian migrant workers there are in the Gulf. There could be some hundreds of thousands of them, possibly over a million, and they are the ones who will presumably bear the first brunt of any retrenchment. Their lack of legal status lays them open to exploitation by anyone with an eye to the main chance, and their defencelessness is likely to increase as the jobs dry up. The seeds of conflict are discernible here, which could at worst result in the rapid repatriation of tens or even hundreds of thousands of destitute people to swell the ranks of the unemployed and discontented in Kerala and elsewhere, an exodus that would dwarf by a factor of ten the expulsions of the Indians from East Africa during the 1960s and early 1970s. Any civil commotion that might lead up to or accompany this repatriation would inevitably result in the involvement of governments, and India's careful wooing of the Arabs would receive a rebuff from which she might take years to recover. And even if the repatriation is long and gradual, as is more likely, unsuccessful returned migrants are likely to prove socially disruptive. Time will in the end run out for many of the legal migrants too, but at least their departures will be orderly and they should have earned enough feathers for their Indian nests to cushion for a while the effect of their return on the Indian employment statistics. The more skilled the migrants the longer will they remain in demand, but even doctors and engineers can fall victim to political upheavals,[66] and will eventually be supplanted by the products of the enormous investment in education which the Gulf countries are at present making.

Notes

[1] I have used the terms 'migrate', 'migrant', and 'migration' to denote temporary emigration.

[2] *Economic Times,* 16 May 1979.

[3] Diplomatic sources in New Delhi.

[4] Quoted in the *Economic Times,* 4 Dec. 1978.

[5] Commerce Research Bureau, *Inward Remittances: Kerala: a Survey* (1978), p. 14.

[6] India, Planning Commission, *Draft Five Year Plan 1978–83*, paras. 3–119.

[7] The Minister of State for External Affairs, Shri Samarendra Kundu, put it at Rs. 1,800 crore (*India News*, 8 Mar. 1979).

[8] James Morris, *Pax Britannica: the Climax of an Empire* (1968), ch. 4, and E. T. Mathew and P. R. Gopinathan Nair, 'Socio-economic Characteristics of Emigrants and Emigrants' Households: a Case Study of Two Villages in Kerala', *Economic and Political Weekly*, 15 July 1978.

[9] Mathew and Nair, p. 1141.

[10] There continued to be large-scale movement *within* the subcontinent throughout the first half of this century, particularly immediately before and after Partition and Independence in 1947.

[11] This information was obtained privately.

[12] Quoted in the *Economic Times*, 4 Dec. 1978.

[13] Commerce Research Bureau, p. 22.

[14] Sashi Kumar and B. Menon, 'Wealth from the Gulf: Dynamics of Change', *The Hindu*, 1 Oct. 1978 ('Weekly Magazine' section, p. I).

[15] Commerce Research Bureau, p. 21.

[16] *Financial Times*, 9 Oct. 1979.

[17] S. Krishna Kumar, 'Overseas Malayalees and Industrialization of Kerala'. (Malayalees are speakers of Malayalam, the language of Kerala, hence 'Keralans'.)

[18] Malayalees are proverbial expatriates, though the higher castes, such as Nairs, rarely broke the Hindu taboo on crossing the sea. There is a popular story which has Hillary and Tenzing reaching the top of Everest only to find a Nair teashop already installed, complete with freshly brewed tea. I have patronized a tea-stall kept by these enterprising caterers at the top of a 10,000 ft pass in Bhutan, fifteen hundred miles and several cultures away from Cochin. Few Nairs or Brahmins have gone to the Gulf, most of the Malayalee migrants being Ezhavas (a low caste), Muslims, and Christians.

[19] Kumar and Menon.

[20] Commerce Research Bureau, p. 18.

[21] National Sample Survey, 27th Round (1972–3), *Provisional Results of Employment-Unemployment Survey*, Oct. 1977.

[22] Commerce Research Bureau, Table 1.

[23] India, Planning Commission, *Draft Five Year Plan 1978–83*, Tables 4.3 and 4.11.

[24] Ibid., paras. 4.25–6.

[25] From 6,000 to 9,400 and from 36,000 to 74,000 respectively (ibid., Table 4.13).

[26] India, Ministry of Labour, *Indian Labour Journal*, 1978 and 1979.

[27] *Times of India*, 24 Oct. 1978.

[28] Information obtained at the Wadi Jizan site on 4 Apr. 1979.

[29] *Times of India*, 29 Oct. 1978, and various 'situations vacant' advertisements in the Indian press.

[30] Commerce Research Bureau, p. 25.

[31] The Ezhavas, known also as Tiyyas, are low-caste Hindus.

[32] Commerce Research Bureau, p. 25.

[33] Ibid. See also n. 18 above. Nairs (a high Malayalee caste) are not present in significant numbers in the Middle East, presumably because, like Brahmins, they are more likely to be affected by caste taboos (such as not crossing the sea) than lower castes.

[34] Commerce Research Bureau, p. 30.

[35] New India Industries Ltd, Market Research Division, *Inward Remittances: Gujarat: a Survey* (1979), p. 9.

[36] *India News*, 8 Mar. 1979.

[37] Information obtained privately.

[38] Commerce Research Bureau, p. 31.

[39] Information obtained privately.

[40] Kumar and Menon. Commerce Research Bureau, however (p. 31), quotes a figure of only 14,000 non-resident external accounts.

[41] *Guardian*, 11 Sept. 1978.

[42] Ibid.

[43] Kumar and Menon.

[44] Commerce Research Bureau, p. 36, the tertiary sector in this case consisting of little shops and food-stalls catering to the needs of construction workers who travel out by bus from the towns to the returned migrants' villages.

[45] To the casual observer, the contrast with the Punjab is marked. There remittances seem to have been invested more productively, for instance in tractors and other farming improvements, or in the mass of light engineering that has sprung up on the outskirts of Punjabi towns, most of it derived from an original connection (manufacturing or servicing) with agricultural machinery. Kerala of course has tiny and largely unmechanizable farms, so the fundamental incentive or catalyst of agricultural machinery is lacking.

[46] Kumar and Menon.

[47] Commerce Research Bureau, p. 34. Agricultural labourers in Kerala were earning more than Rs. 10 a day in 1978, the highest rate in India.

[48] Kumar and Menon.

[49] Commerce Research Bureau, p. 25; Kumar and Menon; B. A. Prakash, 'Impact of Foreign Remittances: a Case Study of Chavakkad Village in Kerala', *Economic and Political Weekly*, 8 July 1978; Mathew and Nair, p. 1147. A No Objection Certificate (NOC) has to be obtained from the host government before a visa can be issued. Migrants recruited directly by firms are spared the difficulties and expense incurred in the acquisition of NOCs, but an unsponsored migrant can pay between Rs. 2,000 and Rs. 12,000 for them, over and above agents' 'fees'. NOCs come in different shapes and sizes, an 'employment' NOC for Dubai or Abu Dhabi at the top of the scale and 'visit' NOCs for e.g. Bahrain or Oman, far lower down. Even these, however, are touted for up to Rs. 2,000, and NOCs have become favoured dowry items.

[50] The company-sponsored migrant will in any case be unlikely to have incurred 'travel expenses' of more than Rs. 2,000, and is thus doubly fortunate compared to his 'illegal' compatriot (Commerce Research Bureau, p. 26).

[51] Kumar and Menon.

[52] *Financial Times*, 9 Oct. 1978, in a report which maintained that the minimum rates demanded were about 25 per cent above the going rates.

[53] *Financial Times*, 26 June 1979.

[54] *Economic Times*, 30 Oct. 1978.

[55] Kumar and Menon, Apparently the agency placed only sixty-seven people abroad, eleven of whom found on arrival that 'their' jobs did not exist.

[56] *Times of India*, 18 Oct. 1978. The occasion was the opening of a regional passport office at Bhopal by Mr Vajpayee, itself an indication of the growth of migration from Madhya Pradesh. Mr Vajpayee, incidentally, recommended that 'more and more' of the citizens of Madhya Pradesh should be encouraged to go overseas for work, but warned them that abroad was 'no place for strikes and hartals. You will find yourselves behind the bars and deported.'

[57] EPI's Ardiya township, GIL's Jebel Ali desalination plant, and BHEL's Wadi Jizan electrification project. See ch. 4 above.

[58] I saw round all these camps. The only tented accommodation that I came across, on an admittedly fairly short tour, housed South Koreans.

[59] 'The Persians' run shops and businesses but are unwilling to risk investment in industry because of Kerala's 'restive' labour force (Commerce Research Bureau, p. 37).

[60] From Rs. 15,000 to Rs. 50,000 in some cases (ibid., p. 37).

[61] *The Hindu,* 21 Dec. 1978.

[62] A record seventy Malayalam films were made in 1977, twenty of them directly financed by migrants working in the Gulf (Kumar and Menon).

[63] Kumar and Menon complain that 'blatant sex and violence, divorced from and irrelevant to the ethos of the environment, are increasingly injected into Malayalam films', and the *Economic Times* of 24 Oct. 1978 cautiously opines that 'the preponderance of sex themes in recent Malayalam movies and works of fiction is attributed by some observers to the heavy demand for erotic from those living abroad away from their families.' These tastes were evidently not shared by those who remained at home. Again according to the same report in the *Economic Times* 'a popular weekly which serialized a novel replete with over sex received condemnatory letters from readers at home, but the letters from the Gulf were uniformly appreciative of the work.' The 'blatant sex' in the films and the 'yellow magazines' would undoubtedly seem very mild by Western standards, but nevertheless they are evidently salacious enough to suggest to some Indian commentators that the Gulf boom has its moral drawbacks.

[64] *Financial Times,* 23 June 1978.

[65] On the other hand Indian migrant workers are doing work of an order of skill which should ensure that their services are required for a good many years yet. It is mainly a question of whether they may, over the next few years, begin to place their earnings, or part of them, elsewhere.

[66] Some hundreds of professional Indians left Iran in the wake of the revolution there.

6

The Record and Future Prospects

A few years ago Indian engineering exports were insignificant. By the late 1970s they had become the country's largest visible source of foreign exchange. Twenty years ago the thought of an Indian firm winning an international tender for a turnkey project in a foreign country would have seemed far fetched. Now such events are commonplace. In 1960/1 India sold engineering goods abroad worth Rs. 10.31 crore. By 1980/1 she hopes to have sold one thousand crores' worth, a target that is to be doubled by 1990/1.[1] Although still a pygmy in world engineering export terms, India virtually doubled her world share in four years from 1973.[2] But what are the chances that she can keep it up? What hope has she of reaching the 1980/1 Rs. 1,000 crore target, let alone Rs. 2,000 crore ten years later?

We have examined India's capabilities and recent record in chapters 2 and 3, and chapter 4 sketched in the supporting infrastructure. In this chapter we shall examine some of the main factors working both in India's favour and disfavour, keeping in mind as a general backdrop the other considerations, such as political instability in her markets, that could so easily throw the most careful calculations and forecasts awry.

The main factors apparently working against India might be: (i) the slowing down of the Middle East construction boom; (ii) the effect on the future capacity and capability of India's engineering industry of the Janata government's determination to boost investment in the small-scale and 'tiny' sectors at the expense of the large houses; (iii) India's lag in technology; (iv) Indian supply bottlenecks and other constraints on productivity; (v) a tendency on the part of Indian enterprises sometimes to rely too much on political factors when tendering; (vi) the lure of the home market; (vii) insufficient credit and other infrastructure backing; (viii) some well-publicized examples of poor performance. Factors apparently working in India's favour might include; (ix) the growing acceptability of

Indian engineering goods and services; (x) government-directed efforts to win India a privileged place in Middle East development expenditure; (xi) India's pre-eminence among LDCs in the breadth of her industrial base; (xii) the ready availability of manpower at all levels of skill. Let us briefly examine each of these in turn.

Apparent Obstacles

Construction Slow-down

As we saw in chapter 2, construction materials and intermediates form an important part of India's exports to the Middle East. And in chapter 3 we saw that Indian construction firms have gained considerable business in the region. A slow-down in the Middle Eastern construction boom should therefore have serious effects on Indian attempts to maintain the growth in her engineering exports.

The Middle Eastern countries, particularly the oil exporters, have been spending enormous sums on construction—over $25 billion a year,[3] representing a staggering 55 to 60 per cent of capital expenditure.[4] It is self-evident that there must be a limit to the extent of the requirements of any country, however rich, for the latest and best in infrastructure, particularly given the small populations and economies of so many of those with which this book is principally concerned. And it is not merely a matter of saturation. By the late 1970s budgetary constraints had also begun to bite. Saudi Arabia, which had certainly not reached saturation point, overspent its revenue of $44 billion by $4 billion in 1977/8. Furthermore some of these countries have established their own construction industries, a development which could reduce the incidence of turnkey contracts won by foreign firms but which, at least until import-substituting industries are firmly established, should itself not affect the level of demand for construction materials and intermediates, though this will of course drop for other reasons.

There are three bright spots for India in this otherwise somewhat gloomy picture. First, the boom has not come to a complete halt everywhere; in some countries (particularly Iraq, Kuwait, and Saudi Arabia) it is likely to continue for a good many years yet. Second, where construction work is likely to continue at a fast pace its nature has started to shift away from crude infrastructure work towards more complex plant construction.[5] Third, there has been a growing tendency on the part particularly of the Saudi government, but also of others such as Libya, Iraq, and the UAE, to stage a kind of Dutch auction among the three or four lowest bidders for a contract, a process which probably favours contractors from developing countries, who, with their lower overheads and cheaper labour,[6] can afford to pare their tenders down further than their Western competitors and still make a profit. In two of the countries (Iraq and Kuwait) where the boom has kept up its buoyancy and seems likely to continue to do so[7] (see Appendix 9) Indian firms are already well entrenched; and the omens should be favourable in Saudi Arabia too as a result of BHEL's good showing at Jizan (discussed in chapter 3). And, as we have seen in chapter 2, India's broad industrial base should stand her in comparatively good stead among other developing countries competing for business in the second, more complex, stage of the Middle Eastern construction boom. The kinds of plant and industry which the Gulf states will wish to establish—for example cement plants and petrochemical installations—are generally well within Indian industrial capabilities, but beyond those of at least some of the other NICs which have profited from the first, infrastructural, stage of the boom. Nevertheless, in cash terms, the Gulf bonanza had probably passed its peak for Indian firms by the end of 1978, just as it had for their Western competitors.[8] The reasons for its decline do not, however, apply to other categories of developing countries in which India has started to develop export markets, such as non-oil producing Arab and other Islamic states benefiting indirectly, through OPEC aid, from the oil revenues boom, and African and Southeast Asian countries pursuing steadier, if more stately, development policies financed for the most part by multilateral aid. Here there is no reason to suppose that Indian exports do not continue to stand a good chance.

Small-scale Industry

The Indian government's *Statement on Industrial Policy*, which was laid before Parliament on 23 December 1977, greatly expanded the list of items reserved for the small-scale sector, from 180 to over 500. The growth of 'large houses' was to be more severely regulated, having, in the government's view, been disproportionate and largely based on heavy borrowing from public financial institutions and banks. Henceforward large houses would have to rely on their internal resources to finance new projects or expansions, which would themselves require specific government approval unless the industry concerned was eligible for automatic capacity growth (broadly defined as basic or high technology industries).

On the face of it this policy might appear to be a severe handicap, difficult to overcome, on Indian private sector firms engaged in engineering exports, directly and indirectly. How does it affect successful engineering firms like Tata, Kirloskar, Kamani, and Birla? Will their sources of investment dry up? Will they be forced out of some of their most profitable product lines?

Before trying to answer these questions, it would be prudent to clear away some potential misconceptions. First, the policy has no effect on the public sector, and many of the firms involved in the activities described in chapters 2 and 3 above are in the public sector. Second, the policy does not apply to services such as contracting and consultancy. Third, there is no statutory reverse or retrospective effect on the large houses, firms already engaged in the manufacture of something on the reserved list being free to carry on with that line. Nevertheless they might find it extremely difficult to obtain the necessary licences and finance to increase its output. They are, for instance, also being subjected to various forms of carrot and stick pressure to persuade them to move out of reserved sectors 'voluntarily'. The method apparently consists of withholding licences for new units or expansions or diversifications in unreserved sectors unless the firm undertakes to give up a certain percentage of its existing production of items in the reserved sector in favour of the small-scale sector.[9]

There is no hard evidence at the time of writing that the policy has adversely affected the export capabilities and performance of large engineering houses. Indeed, as we saw in chapter 1, engineering goods, in which the products of large houses feature very prominently, were exceptional and largely responsible for the continued growth of total Indian exports in 1978/9, which was otherwise a disappointing year. This is perhaps not very surprising, given that most of the products reserved for the small-scale sector (typical examples are matches, soap, and footwear) are for the most part not the kinds of things that would be exported. And even those reserved products which do enter international trade or which could be involved in it are likely to be made by small subcontracting firms under the tight supervision of the large house putting the final article together. Car and bicycle components are a good example, and subcontracting in this way has long been practised in their case.

Much depends on how the policy is interpreted and administered. The areas for large-scale industry (which would include the large houses) are defined as:

(a) basic industries which are essential for providing infra-structure as well as for development of small and village industries, such as steel, non-ferrous metals, cement, oil refineries;

(b) capital goods industries for meeting the machinery requirement of basic industries as well as small scale industries;

(c) high technology industries which require large scale production, and which are related to agricultural and small scale industrial development such as fertilizers, pesticides, and petrochemicals etc.;

(d) other industries which are outside the list of reserved items for the small scale
     sector, and which are considered essential for the development of the economy
     such as machine tools, organic and inorganic chemicals.[10]

There is room for manoeuvre by a small army of company lawyers
here.

The policy recognizes the importance of exports of manufactures
and comes near to making specific exceptions from the provisions
restricting the future role of the large houses 'for export oriented
manufacturing capacity in fields where such investment is likely to
be internationally competitive'. The proviso amounts almost to a
veiled invitation to the large houses to make their proposals big
and bold.

India's Lag in Technology

The December 1977 industrial policy also lays down that the 'future
development of industries in India must be based on indigenous
technology as far as possible' but goes on to recognize that some
sophisticated and high priority technology will still have to be
imported. It favours outright purchase followed by local adaptation,
and firms that are permitted to import will in most cases be obliged
to set up 'adequate Research and Development facilities so that the
imported technology is properly adapted and assimilated'.

Indian exporters, and the government, have laid considerable
emphasis on the appropriateness of their technology, whether truly
indigenous or adapted from foreign designs, for application to the
conditions of other LDCs. Despite the Gulf states' penchant for the
latest and the best, sales of Indian capital goods and engineering
services in the area have steadily increased, and in a perfect world
they should continue to do so in all developing countries, because
there is much to be said, as we have already seen, for the appropriateness argument.

But the world is not perfect. Other LDCs cannot always be
expected to deny themselves the fruits of technological advance,
particularly if the results of Indian R & D (whether of pure Indian
designs or adapted foreign ones) are patently uneconomic, however
well tried and reliable. For the most part Indian enterprises recognize
this (by continuing to go in for industrial collaboration agreements)
but it is not so apparent that Parliament and the government do.
The economic autarky ambitions implicit in the technology policy
quoted above are praiseworthy and have, on the whole, served India
well enough,[11] but when they are taken to the point of blind
technological chauvinism they do India a grave disservice.

A case of what might be termed India's technological autarky syndrome (in which the symptoms of chauvinism are only too clearly apparent) concerned BHEL's attempts to conclude a long-term and broad-based collaboration agreement with Siemens. BHEL had had numerous[12] collaboration agreements with foreign manufacturers in the past from both East and West. Most of them concerned the rights to a particular design or family of designs which BHEL's own R & D engineers then adapted to suit Indian conditions. Some of these agreements (such as that in the Sixties and early Seventies with AEI, later GEC, of the UK for the manufacture of a range of steam turbines) were quite far reaching and comparatively long term, but nevertheless they concerned a particular range of products only. In September 1976 an agreement was signed with Kraftwerk Union (KWU) for the manufacture of larger turbosets, from 200 MW to 1,000 MW. This agreement (like most of the others covering different products signed with many other firms) passed largely unremarked by the press, possibly because it was concluded during the Emergency. But KWU is a subsidiary of Siemens, and in due course it was announced that BHEL had negotiated a much wider and longer-term arrangement with the parent body. A memorandum of understanding was signed with Siemens in June 1978, but, by June 1979, the agreement had still not been concluded.

The object of the Siemens collaboration was to enable BHEL to import a generation of power know-how and establish a system by which this could be automatically updated by the company's own R & D division. BHEL was to have access to Siemens' engineering systems and concepts over a number of years to back up the various single product collaborations (each of which by their very nature embodied a frozen form of technology) such as that with KWU.[13]

But BHEL's management had omitted to take into account the forces of technological chauvinism. The memorandum of understanding prompted a spate of articles in the press (some scurrilous, which we will ignore, others more responsible, such as the leading article in the *Economic Times* of 13 November 1978 which is reproduced in full at Appendix 25 below), the burden of which was that BHEL (and by implication the whole of India's heavy electrical industry) was surrendering its technological independence to a powerful multinational which was in some way conspiring with other multinationals to squeeze India out of world markets. In due course the proposed collaboration agreement was submitted to a special sub-committee of the Lok Sabha Committee on Public Undertakings (COPU), which was chaired by a Communist Party (Marxist) MP with a trade union rather than a technical background. COPU found against the agreement largely on the grounds that it would make BHEL's R & D department redundant and turn the whole company into a virtual dependant of Siemens. It appeared to ignore the fact that the R & D department did not itself oppose the need for an umbrella agreement and did not seem able or willing to believe that BHEL's technology had fallen years behind and could, given the company's slender resources (by international standards), only fall further behind,[14] without a chance to profit from foreign technological advance. The Committee seemed blinded by the company's apparently successful record as an exporter, which they accepted without question,[15] and unable to grasp the concept that there is nothing shameful in profiting from another's technical labours rather than wastefully and possibly unsuccessfully duplicating them.[16] At the time of writing the issue remained unresolved, but the omens for Indian maturity in matters of this sort had if anything become worse with the endorsement of COPU's views by a specially constituted Committee of Secretaries in June 1979.[17]

Supply Constraints

Bottlenecks and shortages have long been an unfortunate feature of the Indian economy, as no doubt they are in many developing countries, particularly if they have large and complex economies. Those which have loomed large in India in recent years have included periodic shortages of steel, power, miscellaneous inputs (especially non-ferrous materials and items), cement (of no great consequence to the engineering industry except as an investment input, but important for Indian contractors working overseas), road and railway transport, and port congestion. A volatile labour force can also add to exporters, difficulties, both directly and through the infrastructure.

To take strikes first, India's record for a number of years has been roughly one day lost per year per employee in the organized sector. It doubled in 1974 and dropped to rather over half a day in 1976 (i.e. at the height of the Emergency). The next year it was back to its customary level, where it remained in 1978. By way of comparison, the UK's record from 1973 to 1978 varied between one-seventh of a day and rather over half a day lost per year per employee. Comparisons of this sort are of course very dangerous, but the difference in performance is so marked that it is indicative of the severity of the Indian strike problem (particularly in view of the UK's own scarcely unblemished record). A more valid comparison can be made with two of India's Asian competitors, the Republic of Korea and Singapore, both of which have negligible strike records. A glance at Appendix 10 will suffice to show how comparatively severe India's labour problems are.

Indian ports are chronically congested. Part of the problem is that there are simply not enough of them, and those that do exist are poorly equipped, lacking much of the modern container and rolro equipment that is taken for granted in the developed world. They are also staffed by fairly militant dockworkers, who do not hesitate to resort to strike action. Indian exporters also complain of a lack of suitable Indian shipping, maintaining that they have to pay extortionate rates to foreign lines to ship heavy equipment to overseas projects. (This may be another way of saying that they need subsidized freight rates to remain competitive.)

Steel is frequently in short supply in India, with a particular crisis starting late in 1978. The government authorized emergency imports, but stop-gap measures of this sort inevitably result in time lags. The 1978/9 shortage was partly the result of a shortage of coking coal which was itself partly due to 1978's exceptional monsoon floods, which put a number of mines out of action. It was also partly the result of power shortages, which were of course also partly the result of coal shortages, an all too familiar vicious circle.

Steel, coal, and power feature with depressing regularity in the saga of Indian shortages. So do cement, soda ash, kerosene, diesel oil, aluminium, and a hundred and one other raw materials and essential inputs. But whereas in the early 1970s the serious effects of shortages of this sort would have been virtually unavoidable, by the closing years of the decade in most cases (power is an obvious exception) the effects could be mitigated by imports, albeit at the cost of some delay, since India had comfortable foreign exchange reserves. And Indian industries, inured to shortages and bottlenecks as a perennial part of the system, carry large stocks and invest heavily in auxiliary generators. Nevertheless exporters were complaining of administrative lethargy: the government assured them they would get the steel needed for their contracts, but these assurances were not followed up at the working level.[18]

Power generation is of course crucial. Auxiliary generators cannot keep major industrial plants at full output, and they are in any case increasingly expensive to run as the effects of oil price increases work through. About 40 per cent of India's power[19] is hydro-generated, a proportion that is expected to drop to a little under one-third[20] by the end of the Sixth Plan period owing to the more rapid development of new thermal (and nuclear) capacity. Hydro power generally has considerable advantages in reliability over thermal power, but monsoon or snow-fall failures can very seriously upset its output in Indian conditions. In the winter and early summer of 1973/4, for instance, the Bhakra dam, which is the mainstay of Northwest India's supplies, was producing scarcely any power at all for several weeks owing to two successive monsoon failures; and, more recently, the serious shortage of power in the early summer of 1979 in Maharashtra (the state which contains the Bombay-Poona industrial belt, the home of much of India's more modern engineering industry) was partly the result of rainfall deficiency in the Western Ghats.[21] Nevertheless hydro power is a better bet than thermal in the long run, not least because of its inherent greater mechanical reliability.[22]

Unfortunately India has yet to develop a national grid (the distances were too great until comparatively recent advances in transmission technology), and the West Bengal-Bihar industrial belt, where most heavy engineering is situated, is far from any significant source of hydro power. It is of course the main coal-mining area (which is why it became industrialized), so in theory there is no reason why it should not have abundant power, provided maintenance standards can keep pace with investment. But capacity utilization is never high enough. In 1977/8 and the first half of 1978/9 it stuck doggedly at 48 per cent; its all-time high, achieved during the Emergency in 1976/7, was only 57 per cent.[23] Indian manufacturers have to bear these depressing figures in mind when they contemplate the otherwise encouraging investment target, which is to increase installed capacity to 44,626 MW by 1982/3,[24] from its 1977/8 level of 24,039 MW.[25]

Over-reliance on Political Factors

India has built up a network of joint economic commissions with Middle Eastern countries (and Libya), and there is a considerable two-way ministerial traffic.[26] Much is made, understandably, of the need for economic solidarity among developing countries and of India's special qualifications as a potential supplier of technology. But it seems that Indian concerns, particularly in the public sector, may at times rely too much on political 'pull' of this sort and as a result pay insufficient attention to pricing and other tendering requirements. The most prominent example of business lost on this account was the Indian bid for the Rs. 1,500 crore Baghdad-Hussaiba railway project in October 1978, which Indian officials were already treating as good as won. A Brazilian firm won it on price, a salutary reminder that LDC economic solidarity is not a fool-proof prescription for Indian success.[27] The Iraqis, despite their willingness to earmark potential areas of activity for India through the apparatus of the joint commission, still attach overriding importance to commercial factors when putting out work to foreign contractors, as do all India's Arab trading partners (with the possible exception of Libya, as we shall shortly see[28]).

It is certainly true that India has won business elsewhere on at least partly political grounds. BHEL's Wadi Jizan electrification project in Saudi Arabia was assigned to India after the Saudi authorities had claimed that Western bids were both extortionate and concerted. (Pakistan, the Republic of Korea, and Taiwan also benefited from the same episode.) But competitive tendering remains the general rule, and the competition will undoubtedly become keener as the Middle Eastern boom either subsides or, more likely, changes its nature, with more firms chasing fewer and technologically more demanding contracts.

The Lure of the Domestic Market

Indian engineering firms grew up in a highly protected market and produced goods to meet the enormous demand created by the rapid infrastructural and industrial development of India. Exporting was never a serious consideration for most of them until the late Sixties or even early Seventies. But it became a very serious consideration— indeed the only option for some firms—when Indian domestic demand shared the general worldwide recession which followed the 1973/4 oil price rise. Markets had to be found somewhere if firms were not to go out of business, and geographical good fortune had already ensured that India was virtually next door to the then only beneficiaries of the oil price rise, the Middle Eastern oil producers themselves. But by 1978/9 domestic demand had begun to pick up, and it became clear that many firms were considering reverting to the easier option of the home market.[29] Engineering exports continued to grow in 1978/9, but the Indian government might have to take vigorous persuasive action to ensure that so encouraging a start should not be jeopardized by the action of opportunist firms. If these were to continue to regard exporting as something to be attempted only as a last resort in hard times Indian commercial reputations overseas would be seriously harmed.

Export Credit Shortcomings

Complaints about export credit are a recurrent theme in conversations with Indian industrialists. They are less prevalent in newspapers, possibly because there is not very much substance to them. Certainly the infrastructure exists (see chapter 4 above) and considerable use is made of it, but it could perhaps be improved by overhauling and streamlining. At the time of writing terms are roughly in line with those offered by India's fully industrialized competitors. Nevertheless exporters complain not only that they are unable to match their competitors terms, but also that the various agencies concerned—banks, government departments, and financial institutions—take so long to make up their minds that the chances to bid for many projects go by default. They also complain that the terms are left to the commercial judgement of the financial institutions and banks concerned, one of the results of which is that the availability and extent of export credit is governed by the cash availability prevailing at the time in those banks and institutions. As we have already noted in chapter 4, the EEPC was pressing for the establishment of a single export-import bank which would have its own resources and combine within its structure all the disparate elements hitherto shared among the various interested agencies, to each of which in turn the aspiring exporter has to make separate submissions. An Exim Bank was, after all, one of the strongest recommendations of the official committee which examined Indian project exports in 1978.[30]

Indian export financing is clumsily organized, and this may have a detrimental effect on actual exporting, particularly project exporting, which the establishment of an Exim Bank could well have relieved. And it is possible that a more coherent approach to other parts of the exporting infrastructure, such as cash assistance, duty drawback, and tax relief, which could well result from the establishment of the powerful central export agency that the proposed Exim Bank no doubt would be, could provide a further useful stimulus to firms, particularly those that in the normal course of events would not contemplate embarking on exporting. But there is no good reason why Indian credit terms and availability should ever have seriously held exporters back; quite the contrary, in IDBI's view.[31]

Some Poor Performance

India's ability to widen, or even maintain, the bridgehead which she has established in the Middle Eastern development market will to a considerable extent depend on the reputation gained there by Indian firms and their projects. The nature of this reputation will also be important at one remove, when developing countries in other parts of the world come to assess the competing claims for a share in their own development projects.

The general impression which the author formed, at second hand, from other foreign contractors operating in the Middle East is that Indian performance is roughly on a par with that of most other developing countries (in practice Pakistan, the Republic of Korea, Turkey, Cyprus, and Yugoslavia). Much of the work is perfectly satisfactory. But there have been some exceptions, such as the delays on EPI's Ardiya Housing Project in Kuwait and BHEL's Tripoli West power station enlargement, both of which have already been noted in chapter 3 above. Delays and cost escalations occur in the best-ordered projects. Often they arise through no fault of the contractor; a case in point seems to have been a hold-up in IAAI's progress on the new airport at Ghat in Libya caused by local shortages of diesel and cement. But when the projects that go wrong happen also to be among a country's largest and most publicized overseas contracts, as was the case with both Tripoli West and Ardiya, the damage they can do to that country's reputation, or to that of the firm concerned, can easily be out of all proportion to the extent of the shortcoming itself, unredeemed by the far greater number of successful, but less glamorous and therefore less publicized projects which go unremarked. This of course is a hazard faced in greater measure by firms from India and other NICs trying to break into markets than by those with established reputations. EPI, for example, was, at the time of writing, engaged on the civil works for the new Ruwais refinery for the Abu Dhabi National Oil Company. Consultants working with ADNOC admitted to advising them to apply particularly critical criteria when assessing EPI's work since, as far as they were concerned, EPI was an unknown quantity. The contract had thus assumed a make-or-break aspect for EPI's chances of any further work in petrochemicals projects in the Lower Gulf which almost certainly would not have applied to nearly so great an extent had the contractor been of West European, Japanese, or American origin.[32] In other words poor performance at Ruwais would incur disproportionate penalties, and EPI knew it.[33]

Apparent Advantages

Growing Acceptability

This is almost the reverse of the obstacle just discussed, but not quite. It has much to do with reliability and quality. But it also has a quantitative aspect—a built-in, self-propelled momentum like economic growth. The momentum was started when India won her first major overseas contract. Provided she goes on winning contracts at an increasing rate her credibility as a supplier of capital goods and technology will remain. But once this success rate drops off her credibility will be in danger of rapid extinction. There has been little risk so far; there has been no doubt of the growing acceptability of Indian industrial goods and services in the Middle East during the last few years. Indeed in certain commodities in some markets, for instance galvanized iron products and cast iron pipes in the UAE, India has established a near-monopoly,[34] and in construction materials and intermediates in general has become accepted as a regular and unexceptional supplier throughout the Gulf. But in more complex goods, and projects, particularly now that the Middle East boom has entered into a secondary, less infrastructural but more industrial, phase of development, India will need every ounce of the credibility gained so far.

Credibility of this sort is largely the result of visible, practical achievement. The Middle East now contains a respectable quantity of infrastructure built and/or designed by Indian concerns, and they are Indian technology's most effective advertisement. The process can of course be helped along in other ways, and Indian officialdom is not unaware of the possibilities. A special 'West Asian cell' was set up in 1978 by the Ministry of Commerce to co-ordinate the Indian government's commercial diplomacy in the area. The economic ministries, worried about what they see as continued Middle Eastern ignorance of Indian technological prowess, have been pressing for an improvement in the size and quality of Indian diplomatic representation in the region. But no amount of official trumpet blowing will counter any lack of acceptability based on the experience of the purchaser.

Commercial Diplomacy

This is the mirror-image of over-reliance on political pull. It is also closely related to acceptability in that it is concerned with commercial and economic diplomacy but distinct from it in that it does not concern publicity work.

As we have seen, the Indian government (in practice the economic ministries) have been active in establishing joint economic commissions with a number of Middle Eastern states, and indeed with all those in the Gulf area, except in the important case of Saudi Arabia. Under this umbrella frequent ministerial visits have been organized in both directions. This institutionalization of economic relations has been taken furthest with Libya, Iran,[35] Iraq, and the UAE, in descending order of effectiveness. In the case of Libya projects are earmarked for India, after negotiation in the joint commission. International competitive bidding is thus by-passed. Small trial orders are placed on Indian firms nominated by the Indian government, followed by larger repeat orders if the trial orders are successfully carried out. In the case of Iran economic co-operation was vested mainly in the Kudremukh iron ore deposits in return for a guaranteed share of the product, but, following the Iranian revolution the status of the Kudremukh arrangements is, at the time of writing, not entirely clear. With Iraq there seems to have been a preferential tendering arrangement for some relatively minor projects. The Indians seem to have believed that the tendering for the major Hussaiba railway project was only a formality and realized their mistake the hard way. In the case of the UAE frequent discussions have taken place in the joint commission about various joint venture projects dear to the Indians' hearts (a sponge iron plant using Indian raw materials and cheap Abu Dhabi energy, a fertilizer plant, a petrochemicals complex, and a drugs factory), but without positive results.

India's Broad Industrial Base

As we noted in chapter 1, India is exceptional in the breadth of her industrial base. Indeed over-diversification, with a consequent lack of opportunities for economies of scale, is a criticism frequently levelled against her. This wide base is the result of a determined and largely consistent policy of import substitution, and it contracts with the road to industrialization taken by other LDCs such as Taiwan, the Republic of Korea, Hong Kong, and Singapore, which have concentrated on making and exporting labour-intensive products rather than domestically designed capital goods. The broad range of India's industrial processes and capacity has bred a wide spread of related consultancy services, in fact more than one hundred firms, some of them among the world's largest. The combination of manufacturing experience and consulting capability over a very wide range puts India into the lead among developing countries (and, some would claim, on a par with some developed countries) in her ability to bid for project-based exports, turnkey projects involving a package of capital goods, plant, and technology. True, there are Latin American examples of integrated export capabilities along similar lines, but within a narrower range. India is out in front in this respect.[36]

Manpower and Skills

India is rich in human resources, far too rich in many respects. But from the point of view of project-based exports she is very favourably placed, more so than any other developing country. Unskilled labour is available in almost limitless quantities, Islamic if necessary. The presence in the Middle East of anything between 500,000 and two million Indian migrant workers is evidence enough of both their availability and their usefulness. The majority of these people are skilled and semiskilled, and a good many of them are qualified (and experienced) engineers and technologists. In 1977/8 India had a manpower stock of nearly 600,000 qualified engineers, 250,000 of them graduates (of whom 6,000 were unemployed), the rest diploma holders (36,000 unemployed),[37] a larger reservoir than any other country apart from the United States and the Soviet Union, and perhaps China. In the Middle East contractors from third countries, who are the major employers of Indians at all levels there, seem well content with their skills and productivity.

The availability of ready supplies of labour and skills is not necessarily limited to Indian companies: the majority of these overseas Indians work for non-Indian employers. It does, however, mean that an Indian concern bidding for an overseas contract in a country short of labour can guarantee the availability of a workforce and engineers. Should the Indian government act on suggestions that the supply of Indian manpower be restricted—by allowing only Indian agencies or even Indian contractors actually engaged in overseas projects to recruit Indians—then Indian firms could be at a distinct advantage. (Though of course the flow of remittances would drop sharply, a prospect that could temper the government's enthusiasm for altering the *status quo*.)

Conclusion and Three Imponderables

An econometrician might be tempted to express these (and no doubt other) factors numerically and work out from the resulting model exactly what India's future prospects as an industrial exporter were. No such attempt will be made here: there are far too many unquanti-fiable issues involved, and much of the evidence discussed above is based on opinion. Nevertheless this factor-by-factor examination, however unscientific, can perhaps help us to see ahead a little more clearly. The results seem to be as follows:

(i)   The Middle Eastern construction boom has begun both to slow down and to change its nature, from simple earth-moving infrastructure jobs to more complex plant and industry projects, most of which are likely to be well within Indian capabilities. As a low-labour cost NIC, India is likely to be more capable of trimming tenders in 'Dutch auctions' than Western competitors. Meanwhile Arab oil money is giving rise to a wider geographical spread of business opportunity from which India is moderately well placed to benefit.

(ii)   The new industrial policy's switch of emphasis to the small-scale sector (see above, p. 66) will have little if any overall effect on the industries and firms which are involved in India's exports of industrial goods and technology. The possibility that manufacturers will be obliged to turn more to exporting in order to obtain their industrial licences could even result in improved export performances.

(iii)   India's technology lag could prove a growing problem. However, some important sectors (e.g. heavy electricals) have shown that they are prepared to take short cuts, provided the technological chauvinists will let them, and since 'appropriate' or middle level technology—at which India is adept—should continue for many years to be saleable in other LDCs, the lag's effect will probably be neutralized.

(iv) Supply constraints are likely to remain a serious problem for some years to come. But they are not overriding since Indian contractors can often purchase elsewhere, and Indian manufacturers have learned to live with them by means of large inventories, stand-by generators, and so on.

(v) Over-reliance on political pull has been something of a problem in the recent past, but the chances are that Indian firms are learning their lesson.

(vi) Many Indian firms still regard exporting as something to be resorted to only in hard times at home. Unless the government can induce them to be less opportunist Indian commercial reputations abroad will suffer.

(vii) Export credit etc. is somewhat confused in India and would benefit from reorganization. But the terms themselves are reasonably competitive.

(viii) There have been some unfortunate cases of poor performance. But those involved in the most publicized cases, EPI and BHEL, have managed nevertheless to go on winning new orders, and have doubtless learned from their mistakes.

(ix) The built-in momentum of acceptability of Indian goods and services is still gathering pace.

(x) Indian economic diplomacy has had some successes, notably in Libya, and, before the revolution, Iran.

(xi) India s broad industrial base is her strongest card.

(xii) The comparative advantage conferred by India's massive reserves of labour and skills is reduced by its general availability.

The composite picture is one of reasonable optimism.[38] But might not Middle Eastern political upheavals, such as the Iranian revolution, or further increases in oil prices seriously queer India's pitch?

The answer to both questions is of course 'yes'. But neither would be an exclusively Indian problem; other countries would be equally affected.[39] It is true that India had a vaguely special relationship with Iran through the joint economic commission and its main manifestation, the Kudremukh iron ore project[40] (over which there has hung a cloud of uncertainty since the revolution) but other countries, including the UK, had their special economic stakes in pre-revolutionary Iran too. Another Iran, say in the UAE or in Saudi Arabia, would almost certainly cost India dear in the short term in cancelled or reduced orders, but it could be argued that in the longer term Third World semi-'socialist' India might acquire a comparative advantage over Western suppliers. We have already seen in chapter 3 how a 'revolutionary' régime like Libya's (and to a lesser degree Iraq's) to some extent gives India preferential treatment in tendering, for what are really little more than ideological reasons.[41] Some Indian administrators and public sector managers are optimistic[42] that India will be accorded similar preferential treatment from Iran once that country has settled down again and resumed planned economic development. They may be right, and the same could go for post-revolutionary markets in other parts of the Middle East. But—ominously—the most immediate and tangible effect on India of any further Middle Eastern upheavals would undoubtedly be a sudden and major exodus of Indian migrant workers. There were comparatively few in Iran, and most of them were at the top end of the skills ladder and thus reasonably capable of finding jobs elsewhere. But the Arab countries of the Gulf contain hundreds of thousands of Indians, including a high proportion of artisan and semi-skilled or unskilled workers, who would be vulnerable in the xenophobia that would almost certainly follow a popular uprising, even if it did not accompany it at the outset.

The effects of further oil price rises are beyond the scope of a book of this sort. Much would depend on their scale and applicability. If for instance OPEC were to introduce an element of differentiation whereby poor countries were to be shielded from the full effects of any further increases, then of course India, which is one of the poorest of the poor, would gain a comparative advantage in the pricing of her exports at the expense of the West. But, in the continuing unlikelihood of any special treatment of this sort, Indian planners and industrialists must presumably take comfort both in the record so far, which shows that Indian industrial exports to the oil-producing countries of the Middle East benefited from the 1973/4 increases, and in the happy chance that India is probably the best placed of the NICs to meet the more demanding technological requirements of the second stage of the Middle East construction boom. And the NICs, as we saw at the outset of this chapter, are probably better able than the industrialized countries to absorb the results of the growing Middle Eastern tendency to pare down tenders by means of Dutch auctions among the lowest bidders.

It might be safer to say that it is impossible to tell how Indian industrial exports would be affected by these two last, virtually imponderable, factors. But a reasonably optimistic prognosis can be constructed for the effects of both of them along the lines sketched above, and that is probably where we had better leave them. However, no such favourable outcome can possibly be predicted for the effects of a third imponderable—political chaos in India itself— but that really is outside the scope of this book.

Notes

[1] These targets are set by Engineering Export Promotion Council.

[2] From 0.12 per cent to 0.21 per cent (EEPC).

[3] Plantecon Overseas (Research), quoted in the *Financial Times* of 22 Jan. 1979.

[4] Economist Intelligence Unit, quoted in the *Financial Times* of 7 Nov. 1978.

[5] *Financial Times*, 26 June 1979.

[6] Ibid.

[7] Ibid.

[8] Farid Abolfathi and collaborators argue in *The OPEC Market to 1985* (1977) for a greater prolongation of the boom than now seems likely, but they also foresaw the switch in its nature.

[9] *Economic Times*, 26 Sept. 1978.

[10] *Economic and Commercial News*, 14 Jan. 1978, pp. 8–9. The quoted passages in the next two paragraphs are from the same source, pp. 10, 9, 10 resp.

[11] by helping to establish the great breadth of Indian industry: see ch. 1 above.

[12] There were twenty-three in force in May 1978 (*Economic Times*, 11 May 1979).

[13] Prem Shankar Jha, 'BHEL-Siemens Accord', *Economic Times*, 10 and 11 May 1979.

[14] Ibid.

[15] See n. 14 to ch. 3 above on the Malaysians' financial estimate of the inferiority of BHEL's technology in turbosets. A further example, also mentioned in ch. 3, is the Libyans' preference for BHEL's KWU-designed equipment for a proposed 4 x 120 MW generating and desalination plant at Tripoli. Furthermore even an Indian electricity authority (the Madhya Pradesh State Electricity Board) was prepared to pay 50 per cent more for a BHEL 200 MW turbo generator of KWU design than for one of BHEL's standard designs of Russian origin (ibid.).

[16] Many Indian economists and technologists would stand the argument on its head by maintaining that the ability to absorb high technology is indeed an indication of that country's own well-developed technological capabilities. Chad, for instance, could not profit from the acquisition from another country of a new generation of, say, generator technology, whereas India (or the UK, or Japan, or any other industrialised country) could.

[17] *Economic Times*, 3 June 1979.

[18] This is the EEPC's view, expressed informally.

[19] Thirty-nine per cent in 1977/8. R. K. Pachauri, *Energy and Economic Development in India* (1977), ch. 6.

[20] India, Planning Commission, *Draft Five Year Plan 1978–83*, Table 10.3.

[21] It was also the result of a failure on the part of the railways to move enough coal (*Economic Times*, 11 May 1979).

[22] Pachauri, p. 112.

[23] *Economic Times*, 19 Nov. 1978.

[24] *Draft Five Year Plan 1978–83*, Table 10.3.

[25] Ibid., Table 10.1.

[26] Some Indian administrators and diplomats find these joint commissions useful points of reference, particularly during the routine mid-term reviews which are held with the host countries. Others, who shall be nameless, find them (or, to be more precise, the one with the UAE) a complete waste of time.

[27] See under 'Railways' in ch. 3 above.

[28] Under 'Commercial Diplomacy' later in this chapter.

[29] Again (as n. 18 above), the EEPC's view.

[30] See ch. 4 above, n. 14.

[31] See ch. 4 above, under the heading 'Possibilities for Reorganization'.

[32] Information obtained privately. There is nothing discriminatory in this. Consultants will always pay particularly close attention to untried contractors, whatever their country of origin.

[33] At the time of my visit to Abu Dhabi, in April 1979, there was no reason to suppose that EPI would do anything other than an excellent job.

[34] According to the EEPC's Dubai office.

[35] That is, until the revolution in Iran.

[36] Sanjaya Lall, 'Developing Countries as Exporters of Industrial Technology', *Research Policy*, 9/1 (1980), p. 14.

[37] *Draft Five Year Plan 1978–83*, Table 4.13.

[38] As a means of quantifying these qualitative judgements one could award them 'marks' (admittedly intuitive) on a scale from − 2 (very adverse) through o (neutral) to + 2 (very favourable), as follows:

(i) + 1	(iv) − 1	(vii) − 1	(x) + 1
(ii) o	(v) o	(viii) − 2	(xi) + 2
(iii) o	(vi) − 1	(ix) + 1	(xii) + 1

This gives an overall mark of + 1, a reasonably favourable prognosis. The markings are of course not scientifically weighted. Once again I can only plead intuition.

[39] This could admittedly just as well be said of factor (i), except that, as I have tried to show, there are special features about the change in the nature of the Middle Eastern boom which India should almost alone be able to turn to her advantage.

[40] See earlier in this chapter under 'Commercial Diplomacy'.

[41] *Economist*, 5 Aug. 1978.

[42] A view expressed to me on several occasions during a visit to Delhi and Bombay in March 1979.

7

The Case of India and Britain

I. EXISTING ECONOMIC LINKS

BEFORE we consider the implications for Indo-British economic relations of India's emergence as an industrial exporter it might be helpful to map out the existing economic links between the two countries. For the purposes of this book it will be sufficient to examine three broad areas: trade, aid, and investment. Other aspects, such as invisibles and reverse technical assistance (i.e. the drain of Indian brains to the UK), will be largely ignored, though naturally they would have an important place in any broader discussion of Indo-British relations. And concerning implications I would draw the reader's attention to my statement in the Introduction that what is true of Britain is generally applicable to other Western countries as well.

Trade

The classic pattern of trade between a developed and a developing country (primary goods swapped for manufactures) has over the last twenty years or so been gradually modified in the Indo-British case. Among Indian exports to the UK tea and cotton textiles, it is true, still loom large, but jute and jute goods have declined in importance while there has been a growth in some 'non-traditional' exports (some of which are in fact commodities) such as leather goods,[1] tobacco (which benefited from Rhodesian sanctions), silver (which fluctuates considerably),[2] garments, and engineering goods. This last item is still relatively insignificant; the UK takes only about 3 per cent of India's engineering exports, but as this share has remained more or less constant and engineering goods are India's fastest growing export it is worth keeping under review. (There could be mutual advantages to be obtained from increasing it.) Tea exports dropped sharply in 1978; the UK was shopping around among other suppliers and the Indians maintained an export tax on tea which was not dropped till early 1979, thus at the time of writing it is too soon to tell whether tea exports will resume their earlier volume. (See Appendix 11 below.)

The overall pattern of British exports to India has changed less over the years. Manufactures have continued to occupy an important place, as have iron and steel (perhaps a little surprisingly in view of India's large and still growing steel industry; one must look to Indian productivity and the mechanics of British aid for some of the reasons), but there is one important and unexpected newcomer: diamonds. And from time to time defence equipment swells some of the categories, as it shortly will again as a consequence of India's agreements in 1978 to purchase Jaguar and Sea Harrier aircraft.[3] (See Appendix 12.)

The principal feature of the trade balance between the two countries has been the Indian surplus throughout most of the 1970s, which reached a peak of over £147 million in calendar year 1976. There was then a sudden switch, and in 1978 there was a £26.5 million surplus for the UK (from exports worth £348.6 million offset by imports worth £332.1 million). This turn-around would have caused more satisfaction in British government circles if it had not been brought about almost entirely by the maverick item of diamonds, up from the already high 1977 total of £70.90 million to £106.96 million,[4] and the sharp and probably temporary fall in British purchases of Indian tea, down from the 1977 total of £113.29 million to £40.26 million. Britain plays little more than an entrepôt role in the diamond trade, adding very little value in the process, and sales of Indian tea might be expected to rise with the removal of the export tax. Indeed UK exports to India of items other than diamonds and other precious stones remained more or less static in volume terms during 1978.[5] The year 1978 apart, we have to go back to the period 1971-3 to find a time when the trend was less firmly set in India's favour, when a combination of circumstances (underspending of British aid, a severe shortage of Indian steel, and the additional complication of the Bangladesh war) resulted in big shipments of aid-financed steel. (See Appendix 13.)

There is little point in a book of this sort in embarking on a detailed inquiry into why Britain, having lost her place as India's leading supplier, has continued to lag behind. This is of course something that has been done more than once by other hands.[6] Suffice it on this occasion to note that she has lost it and that among the more important reasons are the ending of imperial preferences (and their post-imperial hangover, Commonwealth preferences); changes in importers' habits and preferences, reflecting a post-

Independence widening of commercial contact; the arrival on the industrial scene of Japan; shortages of foreign exchange and the consequent strict allocation of import licences according to currency availability (itself much influenced by aid allocations); barter trade with Eastern bloc countries (now on the wane); and the concentration of a country bent on import substitution of capital goods and raw materials to the disadvantage of the once numerous British suppliers of consumer goods. To these must be added the growth in the burden of oil imports (leaving less foreign currency available for the sort of goods which the UK can supply) and the decreasing competitiveness of British exports in general (masked to some extent in the Indo-British case by the effects of aid). The position improved slightly in 1978 from Britain's point of view. (See Appendix 14.)

Aid

Britain gives a good deal of aid to India, during the 1970s more in net terms (net of interest and repayments of earlier loans) in most years than any other donor,[7] and in some years more in gross terms too. (See Appendix 15.)

An outside observer might be forgiven for assuming that this was a natural state of affairs reflecting Britain's former metropolitan role, but in fact it is quite a recent development. In the late 1960s the UK was providing only about 6 per cent of gross aid to India.[8] Contributions were considerably and progressively stepped up during the 1970s, during which two events (the Bangladesh war in late 1971 and the Rajasthan nuclear explosion in 1974) resulted in the drastic reduction of US and Canadian aid respectively, which in turn meant that British flows, which were unaffected by either event, assumed greater relative importance.

Since 1965 the terms of British aid to India have been exceptionally favourable—interest-free, a 7-year grace period, and then 18 years to repay (in the jargon a 'grant element' of over 75 per cent). Since the terms of most of the other bilateral donors were not so generous, at least not to begin with, Britain's net performance soon began to show up in a favourable comparative light even though her gross flows at first remained fairly modest. In 1975 the terms were further eased by a switch to straight grants for all new aid. Debt service was, however, still required on the old loans, but the effect of this was largely cancelled out by the 1978 decision of Britain, in common with most of her 'northern' partners in the North-South Dialogue, virtually to waive repayments and interest on official lending to very poor countries by means of the 'retrospective terms adjustment' (RTA) agreed at the 1978 UNCTAD meeting on indebtedness.

(In the Indo-British case Britain undertook to make available the equivalent of the debt service due—£576 million over the remaining 22 years of the old loans' viability—in additional aid for use on 'local', i.e. rupee, costs.)

Most of the British aid effort has been directed towards industry, though a certain amount has gone into education, agriculture, science, and health through technical co-operation programmes, and some has gone on debt refinancing. Within the industry sector a large but decreasing share has been spent on major discrete projects, including a steelworks, a heavy electrical plant (the core of today's BHEL, including a hefty slice of AEI technology), a number of fertilizer plants, several ships, and a naphtha cracker (the vital core of an integrated petrochemicals complex). Another slab, known as capital investment loans (or grants),[9] has gone towards the purchase of capital goods, in part routed through Indian financial institutions including, in some years, one devoted to assisting the small-scale sector.[10] But the bulk has gone on what most aid agencies would describe as programme aid (Britain calls it maintenance aid) for the purchase of miscellaneous spares, components, and raw materials. (See Appendix 16.)

All this aid, with the exception of the sums designated for debt refinancing and family planning, has been 'tied' to the purchase of British goods and services. Some even was for a while 'double-tied' (i.e. goods from Britain for British firms in India) under an arrangement known as 'Kipping loans', after the then Director of the Confederation of British Industry and their inventor, Sir Norman Kipping.

There is no doubt that British aid has helped Indian industry in a number of ways, by enabling some enterprises to start from scratch, others to expand or update their plant, and still others—in very large numbers—simply to keep going. Many of the firms in this last category will probably have had only the haziest notion that they were being helped by the British taxpayer, since as beneficiaries of maintenance or 'non-project' aid they would simply be aware that they were holders of a particular type of import licence that obliged them to purchase their spares, raw materials, components, balancing items, and so on from Britain. Recipients of 'project' aid on the other hand, who have always been far fewer in number, would in most cases have come into direct contact with the aid-giving authority in the course of appraisals or monitoring. Aid beneficiaries received no direct financial benefit since the object of the aid was to relieve the Indian government of the foreign exchange burden of the imports concerned. Since the firms concerned paid (and at the time of writing still do) the rupee equivalent of the sterling price,[11] the effect of the aid was a commensurate increase in the government's rupee receipts. The resources thus released could then be put to some other use. The general developmental effect was almost the same as the provision of 'free' foreign exchange, but not quite, since the beneficiary firms were obliged to purchase in the UK, when some of them might have preferred to go elsewhere (for lower prices perhaps, or more suitable goods, or better delivery times). At least the balance of payments effect was the same.

This classic pattern of tied aid has caused other headaches. As a result of the rapid build-up of foreign currency reserves that started in 1976 import liberalization measures undertaken by the Indian government have resulted in the availability of Open General (import) Licences (OGLs) for a wider and wider range of goods.[12] The British government began to suspect in these circumstances that Indian importers would continue to purchase from the UK, provided the goods were competitive, whether maintenance aid were available or not, and that therefore British aid would be of more genuinely mutual benefit if it were devoted largely to projects. Meanwhile uncompetitive British goods and the wider choice offered to importers by the greater availability of OGLs resulted in underspending of British aid, project and non-project. The difficulties were compounded in the case of project aid by the increasing ability of India's own capital goods industry to provide the sort of hardware that only a few years earlier had had to be imported.

These difficulties paled into insignificance beside the problems posed by the need to reconcile the British government's official policy, introduced late in 1975, of aid to the poorest[13] with the requirement that the aid be tied to British goods and services. The policy of aid to industry had been founded on official belief in the 'trickle-down' theory of development, current in the 1950s and 1960s but discredited on the basis of empirical evidence to the contrary by the 1970s, whereby the benefits of aid given to industry would trickle down and outwards till they reached all levels and sectors of the economy and thus of the population. (The evidence to the contrary suggested that already rich industrialists simply became richer, as did the urban labour élite, while the rural population remained as poor as ever.) In India's case—and India is the home of more than half the world's poorest people—aid of direct benefit to the poorest must overwhelmingly mean aid for rural development.[14] The snag about rural development projects in India is that they require few if any imported goods; their main requirement is cash, i.e. rupees or 'local costs'. Aid for local costs is of course a form of untied aid, and untied aid against a background of uncompetitive British exports means at best an unproductive swelling of the Indian reserves and at worst more exports for a competitor such as Germany or Japan and thus the export of British jobs. Britain has long recognized the developmental merits of untied aid but has always set her face against a unilateral gesture for these reasons.[15] (If all donors could agree simultaneously to untie their aid the effect should be more or less neutralized.)

This impasse was partially unblocked by two developments in 1977/8. First, the then Minister for Overseas Development, Mrs (later Dame) Judith Hart, directed that a less literal interpretation of Command Paper 6270[16] than had obtained hitherto would permit the spending of aid on industrial infrastructure of the type which could be said to assist rural development, such as electricity generating stations for rural electrification (and more productive mines to feed them) and fertilizer plants, some capital equipment for which was still not manufactured in India. This was admittedly little more than an exercise in semantics, in that it legitimized *indirect* aid for the poorest, but it opened the way to a drive by British aid administrators and industrialists late in 1978 to become involved in the major programme of new fertilizer plants to be fed from the Bombay High (Arabian Sea) gas reserves.[17] Second, Britain's decision to abide by the 1978 UNCTAD agreement on the retrospective adjustment of aid terms means that India will receive an extra £26 million a year in local-cost aid till the end of the century, when the last of the loans will have been repaid. The bulk of the aid programme was, however, likely to remain tied for some time to come. For this and the other reasons mentioned above it seemed—at least until the May 1979 UK general election, which resulted in the return to power of a Conservative government—reasonable to expect recurring disbursement difficulties for as long as a major programme of aid to India remained in being.[18] (See Appendix 17.) But, with the Conservatives, reduced emphasis on the needs of the poorest people in the poorest countries, coupled with their determination to reduce public expenditure,[19] the severity of these difficulties was bound gradually to be reduced. Mrs Thatcher's government, however, has accepted its predecessor's undertaking to reach the UN's 0.7 per cent aid target[20] as soon as its other commitments permit, an undertaking which, given India's size, poverty, and historic connections with Britain, presupposes a continuing flow of aid from London to Delhi on a fairly significant scale.

Investment

Under this heading we shall glance briefly at the various ways in which the British private and public sectors are involved in the

Indian economy. These include industrial collaborations and other forms of commercial transfers of technology as well as investment in equity. It is worth noting also that it is in fact not only the private sector that is involved in this way, for nationalization of British parent companies has meant that British public-sector concerns are now the owners of investments in private-sector firms in India. Ashok Leyland (British Leyland) and Stewarts and Lloyds and Indian Tubes (both British Steel) are three examples.

Britain is the biggest foreign investor in India—for largely historical reasons that need no explanation. According to the Reserve Bank of India[21] British assets in India were worth Rs. 689 crore (about £370 million at the then rate of exchange) at the end of March 1974. The British government put the 1974 total rather lower, at about £275 million, rising by the end of 1976 to about £316 million, or about 10 per cent of all British investment in developing countries. The RBI's figure meant that, at the end of 1974, Britain accounted for 35 per cent of all foreign investment in India (as opposed to 82 per cent at the end of 1948). The three other main investors in 1974 were the USA (Rs. 531 crore or 27 per cent), FRG (Rs. 181 crore or 9.3 per cent), and Italy (Rs. 83 crore or 4.3 per cent). Remittances to the UK (profits, dividends, royalties, and licence fees) in 1976 were worth nearly £54 million, or a 17.1 per cent return on the investment, admittedly at historic cost. Replacement cost would give a much lower rate. (See Appendix 18 below.)

The earliest form of British investment was in trading companies and plantations, but manufacturers began setting up shop during the nineteenth century, mainly in textiles. Mining was another important attraction, as were railways. Many more well-known British firms in other fields arrived in the inter-war years, particularly in the Thirties. Among them were the familiar multinationals of today (though no one used that term then) such as ICI, Dunlop, Lever Brothers, GEC, and Glaxo. The next burst of British investment occurred in the Fifties and early Sixties. This was characterized not so much by new arrivals as by the expansion of firms that were already established, prompted by the requirements of the Indian government's import substitution policies. Since then it has remained fairly static, with little sterling inflow. What new investment there has been has largely been financed by ploughing back profits or with loan capital.

British investment, along with all foreign investment, has been considerably affected by the requirements of the Foreign Exchange Regulation Act (FERA) of 1973. This required foreign branches to convert into Indian companies and limited foreign holding of equity to 40 per cent, with higher limits (51 per cent and 74 per cent) for certain categories such as companies employing advanced technology or exporting significant proportions of their products. Most British firms preferred to expand and diversify (for instance Indian Tobacco went into the hotel business) rather than pull out altogether, and the required dilution has now been largely completed, with little effect on the total level of British investment.

Nationalization has taken its toll, particularly in mining and insurance. Foreign banks were excluded from the nationalization of the banks in 1970, and British banks retain their dominant position among foreign banks in India. Their activities are, however, fairly circumscribed and they are not allowed to open new branches. At the time of writing there are two British (or partly British) oil companies operating in India (Burmah and Shell), but, along with all other foreign oil companies, they are in the process of being bought out by the government, a process which they hoped to see completed during 1979.

The other major piece of legislation which could affect the position of British investment in India is the 1969 Monopolies and Restrictive Trade Practices Act (MRTPA). In theory the government could use its powers under the MRTPA to harass and even break up large houses with major foreign holdings of equity, but in practice this does not seem to have occurred. The government could, however, have increasing recourse to it in pursuit of the transfer of some manufacturing activity to the small scale sector.

India's attitude towards foreign investment has wavered between neutrality and hostility. Despite occasional assertions to the contrary, it has never really wavered the other way towards a genuine welcome. Given the autarkic economic leanings of Congress (probably of Janata too, but coalitions rarely exhibit coherent ideologies and Janata proved no exception), this is hardly surprising. The government has consistently recognized that foreign private investment can play a useful role in the transfer of technology (hence the specially favoured treatment allowed under FERA for high technology foreign firms), but this recognition has always been tempered by the suspicion, common to most developing countries, that the technology thus obtained is likely to be either second best or hedged about with restrictive covenants. As a result the Indians have generally preferred to obtain foreign technology either by buying it outright, or through licensing, under the umbrella of industrial collaboration agreements authorized by the government.

The term 'collaboration agreement', as used in India, can cover a fairly wide variety of means of technology transfer—including the provision of know-how, plans, processes, etc., training in India or abroad, plant and foreign operatives—to enable the manufacture in India of a product developed abroad. It is generally understood to mean a joint venture whereby technology is bought for a lump sum and royalties are paid on sales, but other forms of payment or licensing can be employed, and investment in equity is not excluded, though the Indians would generally regard it as a last resort. Collaborations generally run for five years, but longer periods of up to ten years are now permitted, and, exceptionally, of twenty or even twenty-five years, as in the case of BHEL's proposed agreement with Siemens. They are permitted in all areas of industrial activity unless the item concerned falls under one of the headings, issued periodically by the Ministry of Industry, of industries in which Indian technology is considered sufficiently advanced to render foreign collaboration unnecessary. This ban can, however, be interpreted flexibly with the help of a number of official loopholes.[22]

Indian enterprises had, at the time of writing, entered into more industrial collaboration agreements with British firms than with those of any other country, 1,163 in the twenty years 1957–76, with another 59 in 1977. Britain's share of total collaborations over the same period was 23.9 per cent. The other leading collaborators were the USA with 935 (19.2 per cent), the FRG with 830 (17.1 per cent), and Japan with 443 (9.1 per cent).[23] But Britain's lead was narrowing; in 1969 her share was 27 per cent and the USA's was 17.8 per cent, while those of the FRG and Japan were 15.4 per cent and 8.8 per cent respectively, which is some indication of the way in which Indian industrialists are gradually looking less to Britain and more to the world's technological super-powers for their new designs and processes. Perhaps somewhat surprisingly Britain remained the favourite partner in 1977 with 22.1 per cent of that year's new agreements, but with a diminished lead over the FRG and the USA, which had 21 per cent and 20.2 per cent respectively. (Japan rather surprisingly dropped to 7.5 per cent, having yielded fourth place to Switzerland with 8.6 per cent.) Presumably there is a self-perpetuating element in that many of these agreements are merely renewals of earlier ones, which would partly account for the maintenance of Britain's lead.

About three-quarters of total Indo-British collaborations are in engineering, and this proportion rose to 83 per cent and 85 per cent in new agreements concluded in 1976 and 1977 respectively. Only a small proportion have involved investment in equity in the last few years (10.2 per cent, 3.7 per cent, 7.4 per cent, and 15.25 per cent in 1974, 1975, 1976, and 1977 respectively). (See Appendix 19.)

There is a little Indian investment in Britain, mainly in services (particularly restaurants, banks, and insurance). Birla Brothers used to be involved in an asbestos plant in Northern Ireland, but they sold out their stake. There are of course innumerable enterprises owned by British citizens of Indian origin, but these do not concern us.

II. COMPETITION AND PARTNERSHIP

Competition

Until recently competition in Britain from Indian exports was a concern of almost entirely domestic dimensions. It the nineteenth century Britain supplied India with most of her cotton goods. Although the Indian industry expanded during the first half of this century, it was not till Independence that the pendulum began to swing the other way. The British industry was run-down and at the same time turning more and more towards synthetics. The declining cotton interests were well organized, through the Textile Council, and by 1959 they had pressurized the British government into persuading the governments of India, Pakistan, and Hong Kong to impose 'voluntary' quotas on their exports of cotton textiles to Britain. This was an early example of action taken to protect a 'sensitive' industry.[24] The pattern has been refined and expanded many times since then, with the result that Indian exports to Britain are how regulated by an array of EEC controls and barriers behind whose bland acronymic exteriors (GSP, CET, MFA, etc.) lie months of intra-Community haggling devoted to the protection of a relentlessly growing cohort of sensitive industries in the different Community countries. This domestic competition is a matter more of textiles, footwear, and clothing than of India's more 'non-traditional' exports such as engineering goods (which at present mostly enjoy preferential access under the GSP), but the psychological groundwork has been laid; goods from cheap-labour NICs like India enjoy 'unfair' advantages against which British manufacturers and bureaucrats must be on their guard.[25]

Has the development spread to third countries? Certainly, as we have already noted, India has begun to make a dent in markets which were not long ago regarded as the safe preserves of developed countries by winning construction, turnkey, and capital goods contracts in the rapidly expanding economies of the Middle East. Since one cannot do much to protect oneself from the effects of cheaper competition in third countries, the only apparent option is to despair and pull out, defeated by unbelievably low bids from 'Far Eastern' rivals. The Republic of Korea is regarded as the main culprit, and indeed India is rarely mentioned in this context.[26] But she is in a good position to increase her penetration once the second, less infrastructural, more industrial, stage of the Middle East construction boom gathers pace. The occasional major contract won against British competition, like the Tripoli West power station, could prove the forerunner of larger numbers, and in much more technologically advanced fields (witness EIL's liquefied natural gas project management contract in Algeria).[27] Seen in this light, India's emergence has serious implications for British industry—and of course for the industry of other Western countries.

Opportunities

Indian projects in third countries do not rely entirely on Indian supplies. Supply constraints of various sorts, some of them structural and others at least chronic (discussed briefly in chapter 6 above), force Indian firms to look elsewhere for some of the necessary components and construction materials—often to the UK, since Indian consultants are familiar with British sources of supply and tend to specify them as a result. And of course there are bound to be occasions when some of the equipment is not manufactured in India at all, as in the case of the (American) diesel-powered generators which BHEL was installing at Jizan in Saudi Arabia (discussed more fully in chapter 3 under 'Power and Telecommunications'). The main British supplier at Jizan, British Insulated Callender's Cables, provided the cables. Indian contractors are not under any obligation to procure from India at all costs, though they will do so other things being equal (the 'other things' including delivery and price). Much of the machinery and installation expertise for Star Trading's turnkey contract to set up a textile complex at Zanzaw in Libya was subcontracted to Mather & Platt, and British components and equipment are frequently included in exported Indian railway rolling stock. Even a civil construction project like EPI's at Ardiya in Kuwait[28] threw up opportunities for outside suppliers; the front-end loaders and the hot-mix asphalt cement plant were British,[29] but most of the rest of the non-Indian plant and equipment was American or German. Opportunities of this sort might be regarded as direct benefits.

There are also indirect benefits. Indian domestic demand went through a long sluggish spell until midway through financial year 1978/9 when it began to pick up. Industry was in its own interests obliged—and encouraged—to look to exports, and engineering exports came to assume a major role in the winning of foreign exchange. Partly in order to expose Indian industry to greater competition, and partly in order to enable it to obtain the increased supplies of components and spares that it needed for a sustained export effort, the Janata administration liberalized imports to a considerable degree, as we have seen in earlier chapters, thus reducing the incentives to supply an artificially easy home market, and obliging manufacturers to look instead to possibilities in exporting. But with the 1978/9 increase in domestic demand India's exports as a whole rose at a slower rate in 1978/9 than during the previous financial year,[30] and her foreign trade was in deficit by Rs. 1,062 crore.[31] Reserves continued to grow, however; they stood at Rs. 5,082 crore by the end of January 1979,[32] representing over 11 months of imports covered.[33] So did engineering exports, to Rs. 685 crore[34] (against Rs. 625 crore in 1977/8), though they failed to reach the EEPC's target of Rs. 720 crore. The reasonably encouraging performance of exports in a difficult year, together with the continued growth in the reserves, should have provided the proponents of import liberalization with enough ammunition to ensure that the liberalization measures of 1977/8 and 1978/9 would not be reversed, at least in the medium term. So, the more engineering goods India manages to sell abroad, and the more project contracts she wins, the greater will be her demand for imports of both goods and technology. This point was emphasized by the Indian government and the various trade associations repeatedly during 1978 and 1979, and there were signs that British exporters might be beginning to heed the message. A number of trade delegations visited India in 1978/9, reversing the downward trend of several years. But there was little to show for it in the trade figures, for Indian imports of British manufactures in 1978 did not grow in volume terms, as we saw in Part I above.

Partnership

The Indians have made it known that they are on the look-out for more partners to collaborate in manufacturing in India and in projects and manufacturing ventures in third countries. They are courting anyone with technology in advance of or complementary to their own. If they seem to have devoted disproportionate attention to the British (see the comparisons under 'Investment' earlier in this chapter) that may be the result of a number of factors besides the self-perpetuating need to renew existing collaborations. Many Indian technocrats share a common techno-cultural background with their British opposite numbers; they may have attended British universities or received a British-influenced tertiary education in an Indian university or institute. Indian and British professional associations are closely linked, and the two countries use largely the same technical standards and specifications. In more ways than one Indian and British businessmen speak the same language.

In seeking foreign collaboration the Indian partner will have a number of motives. In straightforward cases with no third-country aspect his main motive will almost always be the acquisition of new, or the updating of existing, technology. He may wish to acquire for his company the *kudos* or other intangible benefits attaching to the use of a brand name or—more likely—the advertising of his firm's close connections with a well-known international name. ('Foreign' is often still a talisman of excellence in Indian commercial thinking.) If exporting is involved, as it frequently will be in view of the preferential treatment accorded to export-oriented collaborations by the government, this 'image' factor will be all the more important, and may make all the difference in his attempts to break into a new market. If the object of the collaboration is a manufacturing joint venture or a project-based export in a third country the foreign 'name', just as much as its technology, may be all-important in winning the host government's confidence.

The foreign partner's motives will probably be more complex. Unless he is planning to take a share in the equity of the Indian company concerned (which is not very likely, but if he is, his motives will be the usual ones of sharing the firm's profits and perhaps of getting round India's import substitution rules), he will be looking for income from licensing fees or royalties or both. Neither by itself will be very attractive; even the two together could provide only a modest return. Maximum royalties can be as much as 5 per cent, but in practice they are usually less. The lump-sum licensing payment is usually about 1 per cent of the proposed Indian annual turnover. Royalties are usually payable for only five years, after which the collaboration agreement expires and the technology is deemed to be owned by the Indian partner. But, as noted earlier, collaborations for longer than five years are now permitted.

There can, however, be more to a collaboration agreement than fees and royalties. In transferring the technology the foreign partner may have an opportunity to sell complete product kits for local assembly. As manufacture picks up, the indigenous content will rise, but meanwhile the foreign partner will very possibly have sold more in terms of components than he would otherwise have sold (given India's generally restrictive import policies) in terms of complete foreign-made products. He may be able to sell training packages. The agreement may be designed to shut out competition, and it may involve the use of a system that effectively ties the Indian manufacturer to the foreign partner for spares and related systems. The foreign partner may be able to take advantage of India's lower labour costs for the products of labour-intensive processes that have become uneconomic to manufacture at home but for which a market at a lower price still exists, and the agreement may provide a source of supply which is closer to some markets than the original manufacturing base. Finally the foreign partner may see the agreement as a way of getting his firm's name known in the Indian market with a view possibly to getting the Indian partner to undertake the representation of other products made by the foreign partner. Meanwhile, of course, the Indian partner has also gained—from the acquisition of the technology.

The successful achievement of a straightforward collaboration agreement with an Indian firm could be regarded as an indirect means of enabling a British firm to cash in on (and enhance) India's ability to sell engineering goods in the markets (mainly in the Middle East, Southeast Asia, and Africa) in which she has already begun to display considerable flair. Third-country collaborations, on the other hand, could be a more direct means of entry. Some of these might, as suggested above, take the form of joint manufacturing ventures, in which case the British firm would take a stake in the equity. Others (and these are what interest the Indians) would be joint projects in which both sides would be joint contractors, or one could subcontract to the other. In either case the motive would be the complementarity of the two parties' capabilities and capacities. A typical pattern would probably involve the supply of the higher technology processes and components from Britain, with the Indian firm providing most of the labour (at all levels of skill), the detailed engineering, and the lower technology components and possibly processes. A consortium approach of this sort could help overcome problems of scale which could put many projects out of reach of either of the two parties trying to go it alone. And qualitative complementarity is *prima facie* more likely to exist between a British and an Indian firm than between two western firms, which are likely to have much the same strengths and weaknesses.

The Indians[35] see Britain as enjoying a great advantage in having a well-established research and industrial base which produces continuously high level technology coupled with the world-wide acceptability of its consulting and engineering services. They feel that their own, complementary, advantages lie in their direct experience of applying the results of their own now considerable technological progress to the development of Third World countries, coupled with their undoubted advantages in cheap and plentiful manpower. They point out, whenever the subject of Indo-British collaboration in third countries is raised, that both countries enjoy certain geographical, historical, and political advantages in various parts of the world, and that in general these do not overlap. Where India has a political advantage, as say in Iraq, Britain still has a technological advantage. A similar political advantage for India in say Libya or Algeria is complemented by both technological and geographical advantages for Britain. On the other hand in countries where Indian 'appropriate' technology might be more acceptable than it generally is in oil-rich Arab states, but which are geographically far from India and lacking in any tradition of Indian trading or settlement, British local knowledge and experience could prove a most useful ingredient in an Indo-British mix. West Africa might be an example. The Indians in general see no reason why, with the judicious exploitation by each partner of its own advantages (which will vary from market to market but rarely overlap with those of the other partner), Indo-British consortia should not provide very strong competition to firms from other developed countries.

Indian businessmen and administrators who think in this way accept that collaboration in third markets is unlikely to happen of its own accord, at least not on any very significant scale. They have made a number of suggestions[36] for an institutional framework, including the establishment of 'consultancy information centres' in India and Britain and of a joint Indo-British consultancy committee,[37] a co-ordinating mechanism to enable ECGD and ECGC to function in tandem when necessary,[38] and even the creation of a giant 'Indo-British Power Projects Corporation', with mixed public and private sector participation, which would undertake jumbo electrification projects in the Third World.[39]

These same Indian businessmen and administrators acknowledge, however, that their enthusiasm has not met with any reciprocal response from the British side. They maintain, more in sorrow than in anger, that British enterprises seem unable to take the long-term view that is necessary for a successful collaborative approach and choose instead the easier (but in the Indian view self-defeating) course of grasping at any immediate opportunities for 100 per cent British ventures. They cannot understand why British firms, with all Britain's historical links with India, should adopt so aloof an attitude that contrasts so sharply with the more imaginative and positive approach of firms from France, Germany (East and West), Japan, the Republic of Korea, Denmark, and many other countries. They complain that British firms expect their Indian partners to pay the whole cost of joint tenders, whereas the Germans and Japanese are prepared to share expenses. They assert that British companies even expect their Indian counterparts to pay their fares and expenses for meetings in Delhi, an attitude which the same Indians say they have never encountered among any other potential partners. British firms are alleged as a general rule to expect 100 per cent British procurement. And, most galling of all, Indian executives complain that visiting British delegations and firms often display a patronizing attitude towards Indian achievements and proposals.[40]

Some of these complaints bear the mark of the over-sensitivity which results from a less than wholly enthusiastic response from friends of whom one perhaps expects too much. Nevertheless there is an alarming frequency and unanimity in these Indian complaints, and a depressing apparent lack of interest among British firms. Those that do show some interest tend, for their part, to complain that their Indian interlocuters are not really interested in collaboration, but simply in plugging the gaps in their own capabilities at minimum cost. They maintain that any British firm which did oblige on the Indians' usual terms would risk endangering the very reputation that had attracted the Indian company's attention in the first place—by association with a project that would stand a higher than average chance of 'going wrong', owing to what British businessmen believe to be a general Indian tendency to over-run or otherwise fail to keep to contractual obligations. There may be something in this last point, despite the exaggerated manner in which it is usually made, in that many of the potential Indian partners (EPI, EIL, BHEL, etc.) are in the public sector and therefore more likely to be able to ride out penalty payments[41] and other unpleasant consequences of contractual failure than their British collaborators, which are predominantly in the private sector and unable to call on government-funded deficit financing.

Somewhere between these extremes there is a happy medium, already found by quite a few Indian and British firms, as we shall see, that use each other's services. But there are few if any signs of a major collaboration in the form of an Indo-British consortium formed to take on a project in a third country, and there seem to have been very few major subcontracts in the kind of development projects which should, on the face of it, be so well suited to joint Indo-British endeavour. The caution of British firms may be understandable, but they would be well advised to keep a careful watch on the activities of some of their European, Japanese, and South Korean rivals.

Any form of industrial collaboration does of course enable the recipient to become a competitor and could be regarded as tantamount to the handing over of jobs. The latter objection does not apply if the technology concerned is too labour-intensive to remain competitive in the West, and the former need hold no fears for an innovative firm strong on research and development. Then there is the consideration that if one firm does not hand over the technology concerned another one almost certainly will. These are arguments to be weighed in the balance by the British firm concerned, which has to exercise its own commercial judgement, for British governments can only advise in matters of this sort.[42] Most, but not all, Western technology is in private hands,[43] and Western governments cannot oblige private firms to hand their processes and know-how to the developing countries—however inequitable it may seem to the latter that they should be deprived of the benefits. The transfer of technology from the West presupposes that the innovator is a willing seller,[44] a point that often has to be explained.[45]

There is, however, a way in which the British government could encourage British firms to participate in joint Indo-British projects in third countries. Major development projects in non-oil developing countries are generally at least partially funded by foreign, or multilateral, aid. To take a hypothetical example: an Indo-British consortium could bid successfully for a fertilizer plant to be built, say, in Tanzania, with goods and services apportioned between firms from both countries. British goods and services used in a hypothetical project of this kind would of course be eligible for British aid. Thus British manufacturers of process plant equipment, possibly short of orders, and perhaps British consultants or contractors (depending on the division of responsibilities between the British and Indian firms), would find themselves part of a mixed marriage of the two governments' devising out of which might grow further alliances in other, richer parts of the world, such as particularly the Middle East and North and West Africa and perhaps also Latin America, less susceptible to official encouragement owing to their non-eligibility for aid funds. These are the alliances—the purely commercial ones—which the Indians believe would, in the long term, turn out to be to the great advantage of both countries. But they are unlikely to be cemented without considerable government encouragement, which can take practical shape on the British side only in the form of official funds, which means in turn that the first experiments must take place in third countries eligible for British aid. Already British aid is theoretically available for the purchase by one developing country of capital goods from another, a form of aid untying that, at least up to the time of writing, has proved virtually impossible to exploit. This proposal, however, does not go so far. It merely seeks to associate British-aided goods and services with Indian ones supplied on normal commercial terms.

Indian Policy and Activity

It is Indian policy, naturally enough, to get Britain involved on Indian terms, or as near Indian terms as can be negotiated, Straightforward (that is, with no third-country involvement) collaboration agreements seem largely to be able to look after themselves, and the Indian government's main involvement with them lies in weeding out proposals which, in its judgement, would run counter to India's interests. Only occasionally is the pressure the other way, with the Indian government itself in active pursuit of an agreement, and then the technology being sought is usually of a fairly spectacular variety (Jaguar aircraft from British Aerospace, for example), But this is not the case with third-country collaboration. There the Indian government plays the part, if not of the suitor himself, then at least that of an active and interested parent intent on securing the most profitable and fecund alliances available, and no opportunity of pursuing the subject is overlooked. A mission by the Confederation of British Industry in late 1976 was assiduously courted. This approach was followed up by a major and well-attended symposium, arranged by the Indian authorities in London in January 1977, devoted entirely to a presentation of the advantages of Indo-British project collaboration. The case was put again to the then Secretary of State for Trade, Mr Edmund Dell, at the March 1978 meeting of the Indo-British Economic Committee, and again to Sir Frederick Catherwood, Chairman of the British Overseas Trade Board, during his visit in November 1978. Other British trade missions, such as those mounted at the end of 1978 and early in 1979 by the British process plant industry and the North-East Development Council, were also subjected to vigorous sales talk on the same lines, even though their intentions in visiting India had been to sell British goods to India rather than arrange industrial marriage contracts in other countries.

Indian administrators maintain that there is a major information gap between British and Indian industrialists—that the former are seriously underinformed, sometimes not informed at all, of the pace and scope of Indian industrial progress. There may be something in this. Certainly expressions of surprise (tinged, one suspects, by apprehension) are a recurrent theme among British industrialists and businessmen who have visited India and been shown examples of modern Indian industry. The 1977 symposium was the first serious attempt to plug the gap, and the posting to London in 1979 of a resident representative of the Association of Indian Engineering Industries, armed with a marriage-broking brief, was another. He was jointly sponsored by the South Asian Committee of the British Overseas Trade Board and was (sensibly) accommodated in offices provided by the India, Pakistan, and Bangladesh Association in the CBI headquarters. Within the first few weeks of his arrival he had been able to make direct contact with a number of British firms and professional organizations that might otherwise never have been reached by the more formal apparatus of conventional commercial diplomacy.

In addition the Indian government-sponsored Engineering Export Promotion Council has for some years maintained an office and showroom in London. And the Indian Investment Centre, originally set up to encourage inward investment only, is now also charged with the promotion of third-country projects, as well as of Indian joint ventures (i.e. outward investment) in other developing countries. Indeed it is designated as the Indian government's 'focal point' for the exchange of information on third-country projects. It also has a London office.

Results

Evidence of Indo-British collaboration so far in projects in third countries is fairly thin. British contractors employ a good deal of Indian labour in the Gulf, and buy a fair amount of Indian materials, but that is not what Indians mean by collaboration; they mean consortia, joint bids, and subcontracting. British and Indian embassies in the countries concerned believe there to be quite a lot of sub-contracting, but find it difficult to put their fingers on actual examples, presumably because in general each is concerned with the promotion of only its own nationals' affairs. We have already noted a few examples (BHEL and BICC, Star Trading and Mather & Platt, etc.) above. Other examples are worth citing. In Libya the British Steel Corporation has taken on some consultancy work from the leading consultants, Dastur & Co., on the big new iron and steel works at Misurata. EIL and the British firm Capital Plant International Ltd put in a joint bid for a petrochemical blending plant in Yugoslavia, though the contract went to another British company.[46] Projects and Equipment Corporation (PEC), the public sector's 'pivotal agency' for overseas projects, was reported[47] to have entered into 'long-term agreements' with a number of foreign contractors, including four from the USA and one, Turriff International, from the UK. PEC was said to be hoping that the PEC-Turriff combine would lead to contracts in the petroleum and pipeline fields, while the Indo-US combines would concentrate more on water and sewage projects. The PEC-Turriff 'long-term agreement' was, however, merely an unwritten understanding that the two firms might co-operate in the future. It grew out of a one-off joint bid for a pipeline job in India that in fact did not succeed. Nevertheless PEC is well established as a subcontractor to certain other, American, firms working on major projects in Saudi Arabia and Iraq, PEC's role being that of materials and equipment supplier.

Indian consultants take on quite a lot of work from British engineering firms. Tata Consulting Engineers, for instance, collaborate in this way with British firms such as Halcrows, Ewbank, and Sirycon, generally as subcontractors but sometimes also as equal partners, and EIL has been doing design engineering work for Lummus (UK) on heat exchangers for export to the Soviet Union. Other British firms using Indian services in this way include Clarke Chapman, Kennedy & Donkin, and Plessey, and Tata Exports has manufactured equipment for British Insulated Callender's Cables. No doubt there are many more isolated examples of this kind, but so far there has not been a major identifiably Indo-British development project in a third country.[48]

Notes

[1] As distinct from unfashioned leather, which has long been a 'traditional' export.

[2] And the export of which was banned early in 1979.

[3] The Jaguar agreement involves the manufacture in India by Hindustan Aeronautics Ltd of Jaguar strike and training aircraft under licence, with the gradual stepping up of the indigenous content. The first aircraft will, however, be imported ready-built. The Harrier agreement is for purchase of a limited number of ready-built Sea Harrier vertical take-off aircraft.

[4] 25.5 per cent and 30.7 per cent of total British exports to India in 1977 and 1978 respectively.

[5] UK exports to India for the period Jan.-Sept. 1978 amounted to £241 million, against £203 million for the same period in 1977, a current price increase of 19 per cent, or 10 per cent in volume terms after taking account of the 9 per cent increase in British export prices. Excluding diamonds and other precious stones, exports grew in current prices by 11 per cent (from £131 million to £147 million). Unfortunately the corresponding price index also grew by 11 per cent.

[6] Notably by Michael Lipton and John Firn in *The Erosion of a Relationship: India and Britain since 1960.*

[7] i.e. bilateral donor. The World Bank's 'soft' aid affiliate, the International Development Association, gives far more.

[8] Lipton and Firn, p. 97.

[9] Since 1975 all British aid to very poor countries, India included, has been in grant form. The last loans, which had a maturity of 25 years, were provided in that year, which means that all repayments should be completed at the turn of the century. Repayments and interest in the meantime will

effectively be neutralized by means of retrospective terms adjustment (RTA), on which see below.

[10] The National Small Industries Corporation (NSIC). The other institutions are the Industrial Credit and Investment Corporation of India Ltd (ICICI) and the Industrial Finance Corporation of India (IFCI).

[11] Unless, as has very occasionally happened, the Indian government chooses not to pass on the full rupee cost to the firm.

[12] Discussed further in ch. 1 above, particularly n. 15.

[13] Great Britain, Ministry of Overseas Development, *Overseas Development. The Changing Emphasis in British Aid Policies: More Help for the Poorest* (Oct. 1975, Cmnd 6270) defined (pp. 7 and 8) the three 'legs' of British aid strategy thus: (i) 'to give an increasing emphasis in our bilateral aid towards the poorest countries, espcially those in this group most seriously affected by the rise in the price of oil and other commodities;' (ii) 'to promote situations in which British concessional aid funds can stimulate matching contributions of concessional funds from other governments, and to encourage the deployment of such aid through both multilateral and bilateral channels towards the poorest countries;' (iii) 'not only to put a new emphasis on programmes oriented towards the relief of poverty . . . but to give a special emphasis to rural development.'

[14] It can of course also mean aid for the urban poor, but the British government has found few satisfactory means of spending aid money on urban *development,* of the type that would directly benefit the poorest urban dwellers, as opposed to e.g. famine relief.

[15] The members of the OECD's Development Assistance Committee (DAC)—i.e. the main aid givers of the industrialized world—have made many attempts at achieving a multilateral agreement to untie their aid, so far with very little success.

[16] See n. 13 above.

[17] Cynics might say that the production of fertilizer benefits only the bigger and richer farmers, since very poor farmers lack the capital or creditworthiness to buy enough of it to make any difference to the fertility of their land. The UK House of Commons Select Committee on Overseas Development, in its 1978/9 session, pointed to the further risk that one of the effects of the provision of fertilizer was an increase in agricultural labour-intensification and hence greater rural unemployment. (*The Pattern of UK Aid to India,* House of Commons paper 338, 1979, p. xxiii.)

[18] The position seemed, however, to have improved in 1978/9 and 1979/80, with a switch towards a tendency to overspend.

[19] Aid was included in the new government's first instalment of public expenditure reductions, with a cut of £50 million for 1979/80 (on a global basis).

[20] Whereby aid donors (with some notable exceptions, including the USA and the USSR) are pledged to transfer 0.7 per cent of their GNPs as official

development assistance. By 1979 only three countries had met this 'Pearson target'. Britain managed 0.52 per cent in 1979.

[21] RBI, *Bulletin,* Mar. 1978.

[22] The Indian government's illustrative list and explanation of exemptions is summarized as follows in *Economic and Commercial News,* 6 Jan. 1979, pp. 11–12:

Areas of Foreign Investment and Collaboration Defined

In para. 25 of the Statement on Industrial Policy laid down before the Parliament by the Minister of Industry on December 23, 1977, it was stated that to guide entrepreneurs, Government will issue a revised illustrative list of industries where no foreign collaboration, financial or technical is considered necessary since indigenous technology has fully developed in this field.

Accordingly, such a list has been prepared for the guidance of the entrepreneurs (list given below). This list will replace the lists of industries, issued by Government in 1969, viz (a) list of industries where foreign investment may be permitted; (b) list of industries where only foreign technical collaboration may be permitted (but not foreign investment); and (c) the list of industries where no foreign collaboration (financial or technical) is considered necessary.

It is clarified that the list of industries, given below, is only illustrative. A broad technology base has already been established in the country. But, with constant technological advancements taking place in the developed countries, the need to update India's production technology would arise in almost all industries over a period of time. The Administrative Ministries/Foreign Investment Board may therefore consider import of technology even in these fields if—

(i) indigenous technology for items in the list developed/exported is too closely held and is not available for use by new entrepreneurs on competitive terms;

(ii) technology is required for updating of existing technology in India to meet efficiently domestic requirements or to become competitive in the export market;

(iii) such import is required for manufacture of items with substantial exports backed by buy-back guarantees.

In order to streamline and further expedite the procedures for securing approvals relating to foreign collaboration proposals, Government have decided to delegate additional powers to the Administrative Ministries to accord approvals for foreign collaboration proposals subject to the following conditions:

(1) There is no foreign equity participation in the proposal.

(2) The applicant is not a company with existing foreign equity investment.

(3) The item proposed to be manufactured is consistent with the priorities set out in the Industrial Policy Statement.

(4) The foreign exchange outgo in case of lumpsum, if any, and royalty together should not exceed Rs. 5 million in the aggregate.

Secretariat of Industrial Approvals (SIA) will continue to provide the centralised secretariat for all foreign investment and/or collaboration approvals. Therefore, all applications for foreign investment and/or collaboration will continue to be made to the Secretariat of Industrial Approvals in the Department of Industrial Development, Ministry of Industry, Udyog Bhavan, New Delhi, as hitherto.

The following is the illustrative list, and not exhaustive, of industries where no foreign collaboration, financial or technical, is considered necessary:

Metallurgical industries: ferrous-ordinary castings, bright bars, structurals, welded CI steel pipes and tubes; and non-ferrous—antimony, sodium metal, electrical resistance heating (nickel free alloy), aluminium litho plates.

Electrical equipment: electrical fans, common domestic appliances, common types of winding wires and strips, iron clad switches, AC motors, cables and distribution transformers.

Electronic components and equipment: general purpose transistors and diodes, paper, mica and variable capacitors, TV receivers, tape recorders, teleprinters, PA systems, record players/changers.

Scientific and industrial instruments: non-specialised types of valves, meters, weighing machinery and mathematical surveying and drawing instruments.

Transportation: railway wagons, bicycles.

Industrial machinery: building and constructional machinery, oil mill machinery, conventional rice mill machinery, sugar machinery, tea processing machinery, general purpose machinery.

Machine tools: forged hand tools, general purpose machine tools.

Agricultural machinery: tractor-drawn implements, power tillers, foodgrain dryers, agricultural implements.

Miscellaneous mechanical engineering industries.

Commercial, office and household equipments of common use.

Medical and surgical applicances.

Fertilizers: single superphosphate and granulated fertilizers.

Chemicals (other than fertilizers): [various].

Dyestuffs: [various].

Drugs and pharmaceuticals: [various].

Paper and pulp including paper products.

Consumer goods.

Vegetable oils and vanaspati.

Rubber industries: viscose tyre yarn, metal bonded rubber, latex foam, rubberised fabrics, bicycle tyres and tubes.

Leather, leather goods and pickers: belting-leather, cotton and hair finished leather, pickers, picking bands, vegetable tanning extracts, fat liquors other than synthetic.

Glass and ceramics.

Cement and gypsum products.

[23] Tata Services Ltd, *Statistical Outline of India 1978*.

[24] Lipton and Firn, ch. 4.

[25] For an exhaustive discussion of the access barriers facing Indian exports to the UK and other members of the EEC see Vincent Cable and Ann Weston, *South Asia's Exports to the EEC—Obstacles and Opportunities* (1979).

[26] *The Times*, 19 Oct. 1978, and *Financial Times*, 22 Jan. and 26 June 1979.

[27] Discussed under Petroleum and Chemicals' in ch. 3 above.

[28] See under 'Construction: Civil and Structural Engineering' in ch. 3 above.

[29] As are 45,271 brass mortice locks.

[30] Rs. 5,544 crore (provisional) for 1978/9, as against Rs. 5,253 crore for 1977/8, a very creditable performance when it is recalled that 1978/9's exports were running behind 1977/8's as late as Dec. 1978 (*Economic Times*, 16 May 1979).

[31] Provisional figure (*Economic Times*, 27 May 1979).

[32] *Economic and Commercial News*, 5 May 1979.

[33] *International Finance* (Chase Manhattan Bank), 11 June 1979.

[34] Provisional figure (*Economic Times*, 12 June 1979).

[35] By 'the Indians' I mean here and in other places made clear by the context the many people involved in industrial exporting whom I met in Delhi and Bombay, and in the Gulf countries, in March and April 1979. They were for the most part senior executives in public and private sector firms, engineers, economists, bankers, civil servants, diplomats, and project managers. I do not mean necessarily to imply an official opinion.

[36] Particularly during the symposium referred to on p. 101 above.

[37] These are the suggestions of Mr Kan D. Mariwalla, the Chairman and Managing Director of the NIDC, who is one of the leading proponents of Indo-British collaboration in third markets.

[38] A particular concern of Mr M. M. Luther, the Chairman of PEC.

[39] An idea worked out in considerable detail by Mr M. Dhar, the Managing Director of Kamani Engineering.

[40] These views were expressed to me with particular vigour by EPI, but I heard them from a depressingly large number of the other firms and associations where I held interviews.

[41] Some of the big Indian public-sector companies, such as for example EPI, make no bones about their 'loss leader' approach to overseas business.

[42] While Indian governments can, as we saw in Part I of this chapter, give a certain direction to collaborations through the banned industries list and the need for all collaboration agreements to be approved.

[43] Exceptions would occur in e.g. nuclear and aerospace engineering.

[44] A happy turn of phrase taken from Sir T. Garvey's *Bones of Contention* (London, Routledge & Kegan Paul, 1978), p. 127.

[45] As it had to be with some force at the Indo-EEC seminar in Feb. 1979 (*The Hindu*, 7 Feb. 1979).

[46] The reason is alleged to have been that the Yugoslavs distrusted the notion of taking technology from another developing country, so they accepted the second-best tender.

[47] *Economic and Commercial News*, 11 Mar. 1978.

[48] Ways in which further progress could be made might include the following: (i) British firms should take advantage of Indian attempts to bridge the information gap. Without a focal point collaboration in third countries is bound to be a hit-and-miss affair, but AIEI's permanent representation in London should make it easier to open up channels of communication and alert potential partners to opportunities before it is too late. The UK Department of Trade should encourage firms to consult the AIEI and the IIC; (ii) British and Indian embassies and high commissions in appropriate countries (initially in the Middle East, Southeast Asia, and Africa, but later perhaps also in Latin America and elsewhere in the developing world) could be instructed to keep in close touch with a view to identifying projects suitable for Indo-British collaboration. It is significant that few of the Indian diplomatic posts consulted in the course of this research seemed very aware of the government of India's enthusiasm for Indo-British collaboration; (iii) the British government should give serious consideration to ways in which British aid (capital and technical) could be used to help finance Indo-British joint projects in other developing countries, to the benefit of all three countries involved in each project, and with a view to encouraging further collaboration in other, richer countries not eligible for British aid, especially in the Middle East and North and West Africa, and perhaps also in Latin America.

8

Envoi

It is not many years since the products of Japanese industry were regarded in the developed West as cheap imitative items not worth buying. A trace of the same attitude is still displayed towards the products of other newly industrialized countries such as Taiwan and Hong Kong, but less and less as the popular myths of Western industrial hegemony are exploded. It is unlikely that Indian consumer goods will ever flood the markets of the older industrialized world (though, given a few more years of oil shortages, Indian scooters could well prove highly popular), but Indian-made components will probably be incorporated into Western equipment on an increasing scale. And, more visibly, there is every reason to suppose that Indian contracting and capital goods will make greater and more impressive inroads into markets in other developing countries which hitherto European and American firms have had largely to themselves.

India's ability to undertake major development projects is now well proven. No doubt the needs of India's own development will continue to absorb a high proportion of her contracting and engineering industries. But these industries have grown rapidly, and inevitably a time will come (it may already have arrived) when capacity in these areas will have permanently outstripped domestic demand, particularly since there must be a point—admittedly still fairly distant—at which India's infrastructural needs are largely satisfied. Furthermore both industry and government have tasted the fruits of exporting and found them, though for different reasons, to their taste. So India's presence on the international project scene is unlikely to be a temporary phenomenon.

The arrival of a new foreign competitor enjoying the advantages of cheap labour, low overheads, and newer equipment may have come as a shock. It could still be met, GATT and other international policemen notwithstanding, by retiring behind a newly erected or enhanced barricade of quotas, tariffs, 'voluntary' restrictions, and so on. Clearly, however, a country cannot offer that protection in the territory of another. If its firms cannot compete in third markets they must simply give up, as a number of British and other Western contractors have found in the past three or four years in the Gulf.

There is, however, an old adage 'If you can't beat them, join them,' which potential victims of this competition might do worse than to consider. Indian manufacturers, consultants, and contractors, despite all the rebuffs they have received, are still anxious to collaborate with British firms in third-market projects. And indeed an Indo-British consortium approach could be a very powerful one in a world of larger but fewer development projects. But so could a consortium of firms from India and the Federal Republic of Germany or India and the Republic of Korea, even more so, and they could well be the alternatives, for the Indians are set on finding a major partner.

Appendices

Appendix 1   Indian Reserves of Foreign Exchange, Gold, and SDRs:
Selected Dates in the 1970s

A

	Nov. 76	Nov. 77	June 78	July 78	Aug. 78	Sept. 78	Oct. 78	Nov. 78
Foreign exchange and gold (Rs. crore)	2403	4180	4733	4594	4789	4820	4945	5153
SDRs (million)	197	144	177	184	195	221	221	226

Source: Compiled from *Reserve Bank of India Bulletin,* Nov. 1978.

B

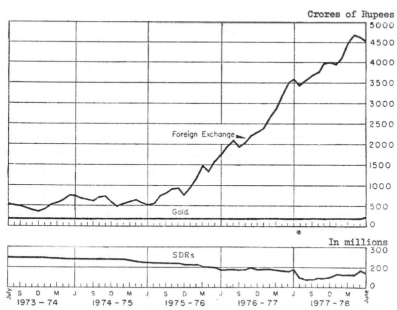

Source: Reserve Bank of India, *Annual Report 1977–78* (supplement to the *Bulletin,* June 1978), facing p. 10.

Appendix 2 Major Items of Indian Exports 1974–5 to 1976–7

Item	1974–5		1975–6		1976–7	
	Rs. crore	Per cent to total	Rs. crore	Per cent to total	Rs. crore	Per cent to total
Iron and steel items	88.39	2.66	121.50	3.02	387.62	7.78
Cotton manufactures	215.11	6.46	216.17	5.37	331.32	6.65
Clothing	138.36	4.16	202.78	5.04	325.04	6.53
Non-metallic mineral manufactures	123.88	3.72	187.12	4.65	310.27	6.23
Tea	228.06	6.85	236.92	5.88	292.97	5.88
Feeding stuff for animals	103.53	3.11	106.62	2.65	256.53	5.15
Leather	133.88	4.02	191.46	4.76	246.30	4.94
Iron ore and concentrates	160.39	4.82	213.93	5.31	238.49	4.80
Jute manufactures	294.03	8.83	247.84	6.16	197.46	3.96
Fish and fish preparations	65.00	1.95	125.89	3.13	178.23	3.58
Non-ferrous metals	90.64	2.72	201.96	5.02	178.15	3.57
Fruits and vegetables	137.03	4.12	132.60	3.29	158.24	3.18
Sugar	339.86	10.21	474.93	11.80	150.07	3.01
Metal manufactures	68.52	2.06	82.07	2.04	132.09	2.65
Non-electrical machinery	91.43	2.75	108.51	2.70	119.64	2.40
Coffee	51.36	1.54	66.65	1.66	114.05	2.29
Tobacco, unmanufactured	80.36	2.41	93.13	2.31	96.62	1.94
Transport equipment	66.62	2.00	83.54	2.07	95.06	1.91
Crude vegetable materials	89.53	2.69	71.62	1.78	83.90	1.68
Electrical machinery	57.46	1.73	64.33	1.60	83.79	1.68
Floor coverings, tapestries, etc.	43.55	1.31	49.55	1.23	76.66	1.54
Spices	61.41	1.85	71.52	1.78	72.92	1.46
Oilseeds, nuts and kernels	29.28	0.88	82.20	2.04	71.15	1.43
Textile yarn and thread	37.64	1.13	22.81	0.57	54.56	1.10
Art collectors' pieces	34.09	1.02	34.88	0.87	52.21	1.05
Ores and concentrates of non-ferrous metals	30.44	0.92	43.94	1.09	49.40	0.99
Fixed vegetable oils	33.66	1.01	35.62	0.88	48.58	0.98
Crude minerals	28.93	0.87	27.62	0.69	33.39	0.67
Textile fabrics, woven	27.70	0.83	24.75	0.61	41.02	0.82
Raw cotton	17.05	0.51	47.20	1.17	38.74	0.78

Appendix 2—cont'd.

Item	1974–5		1975–6		1976–7	
	Rs. crore	Per cent to total	Rs. crore	Per cent to total	Rs. crore	Per cent to total
Dyeing, tanning and colouring materials	23.21	0.70	18.92	0.47	33.25	0.67
of which: Synthetic organic dyestuff	13.87	0.42	10.30	0.26	23.85	0.48
Pigments, paints, etc.	9.21	0.28	8.13	0.20	8.90	0.18
Crude rubber and rubber manufactures	25.72	0.77	11.26	0.28	30.65	0.62
Footwear	20.76	0.62	22.06	0.55	29.57	0.59
Medical and pharmaceutical products	22.96	0.69	22.71	0.56	23.42	0.47
Crude animal material	27.20	0.82	15.85	0.39	22.64	0.45
Wood, lumber and cork	9.41	0.28	13.23	0.33	19.21	0.39
Petroleum products	13.63	0.41	19.99	0.50	18.36	0.37
Meat and meat preparations	5.25	0.16	11.00	0.27	17.88	0.36
Cereals and cereal preparations	25.09	0.76	19.28	0.48	17.69	0.36
of which: Rice	21.50	0.65	13.04	0.32	6.12	0.12
Coal, coke and briquettes	6.80	0.20	17.05	0.42	14.34	0.29
Perambulators, toys, games and sporting goods	7.89	0.24	8.27	0.20	12.81	0.26
Organic chemicals	8.02	0.24	7.39	0.18	11.38	0.23
Wood and cork manufactures (excluding furniture)	8.35	0.25	6.02	0.15	11.47	0.23
Inorganic chemicals	19.11	0.57	8.06	0.20	9.12	0.18
Others	138.24	4.15	155.17	4.85	194.84	3.90
Total	3,328.83	100.00	4,025.92	100.00	4,981.01	100.00

Note: Commodities are ranked according to the last column.

Source: Economic Monitoring Service, *Foreign Trade Statistics of India 1978.*

Appendix 3   Destination of Indian Exports 1974–5 to 1976–7

Exports to	1974–5		1975–6		1976–7	
	Rs. crore	Per cent to total	Rs. crore	Per cent to total	Rs. crore	Per cent to total
USA	374.93	11.26	517.63	12.86	549.58	11.03
Japan	296.65	8.91	432.21	10.74	540.23	10.85
UK	312.26	9.38	419.78	10.43	510.12	10.24
USSR	421.35	12.66	416.69	10.35	440.39	8.84
West Germany	106.17	3.19	117.41	2.92	224.33	4.50
Netherlands	71.75	2.16	82.06	2.04	185.70	3.73
France	86.32	2.59	85.74	2.13	161.82	3.25
Iran	214.84	6.45	272.24	6.76	144.94	2.91
Dubai	40.18	1.21	55.70	1.38	135.23	2.71
Italy	52.43	1.58	79.83	1.98	116.69	2.34
Kuwait	38.40	1.15	47.04	1.17	113.04	2.27
Poland	77.47	2.33	88.37	2.20	112.47	2.26
Belgium	52.66	1.58	45.36	1.13	98.06	1.97
Egypt	52.55	1.58	100.13	2.49	90.77	1.82
Saudi Arabia	35.55	1.07	60.13	1.49	75.08	1.51
Hong Kong	27.84	0.84	44.05	1.09	72.14	1.45
Switzerland	16.33	0.49	58.50	1.45	69.19	1.39
Australia	66.41	1.99	48.19	1.20	64.69	1.30
Indonesia	50.94	1.53	51.72	1.28	60.65	1.22
Singapore	37.48	1.13	52.96	1.32	57.82	1.16
Bangladesh	42.23	1.27	62.18	1.54	54.57	1.10
Sudan	66.46	2.00	36.52	0.91	51.15	1.03
Nepal	42.40	1.27	50.96	1.27	50.65	1.02
Yugoslavia	29.74	0.89	29.30	0.73	49.33	0.99
Canada	44.18	1.33	45.73	1.14	48.70	0.98
Iraq	72.86	2.19	63.81	1.58	46.55	0.93
Yemen Arab Republic	16.16	0.49	16.18	0.40	44.53	0.89
Czechoslovakia	60.38	1.81	34.60	0.86	43.19	0.87
East Germany	34.76	1.04	25.87	0.64	42.47	0.85
Sri Lanka	26.85	0.81	23.10	0.57	39.03	0.78

Appendix 3—cont'd.

Exports to	1974–5		1975–6		1976–7	
	Rs. crore	Per cent to total	Rs. crore	Per cent to total	Rs. crore	Per cent to total
Romania	24.06	0.72	54.52	1.35	38.26	0.77
Oman	16.71	0.50	19.44	0.48	30.00	0.60
Malaysia	29.26	0.88	32.82	0.82	29.84	0.60
Thailand	12.35	0.37	17.13	0.43	25.65	0.51
Sweden	15.78	0.47	13.26	0.33	25.47	0.51
Abu Dhabi	4.56	0.14	10.55	0.26	25.44	0.51
Nigeria	21.88	0.66	37.42	0.93	24.97	0.50
Tanzania	9.79	0.29	16.62	0.41	24.00	0.48
Denmark	9.70	0.29	11.64	0.29	23.92	0.48
Bahrain	9.48	0.28	17.01	0.42	23.49	0.47
Philippines	4.01	0.12	11.67	0.29	22.63	0.45
Bulgaria	17.12	0.51	22.87	0.57	21.97	0.44
Afghanistan	14.83	0.45	34.39	0.85	21.60	0.43
Hungary	19.51	0.59	14.25	0.35	21.14	0.42
Qatar	8.61	0.26	9.88	0.25	19.30	0.39
Kenya	15.40	0.46	15.71	0.39	17.53	0.35
Other countries	227.25	6.83	222.75	5.53	292.69	5.90
Total	3,328.83	100.00	4,025.92	100.00	4,981.01	100.00

Note: Countries are ranked according to the last column.

Source: As Appendix 2 above.

Appendix 4   Indian Engineering Exports: Selected Years 1966–7 to 1977–8 (Rs. crore)

	1966–7		1968–9		1970–1		1972–3		1974–5		1975–6		1976–7		1977–8[a]	
	Amount	%	Amount	%	Amount	%	Amount	%	Amount	%	Amount	%	Amount	%	Amount	%
(i) Total exports	862.05	(100.0)	1357.87	(100.0)	1535.16	(100.0)	1970.84	(100.0)	3328.83	(100.0)	4042.81	(100.0)	5143.23	(100.0)	5253.00	(100.0)
(ii) Total engineering exports	30.70	(3.6)	84.41	(6.2)	115.76	(7.5)	141.08	(7.2)	349.11	(10.5)	408.22	(10.1)	551.68	(10.7)	625.00	(11.9)
(iii) of which, total engineering exports to Iran, Iraq, Kuwait, Libya, Oman, Qatar, Saudi Arabia, UAE	5.81	(18.9)[b]	20.37	(24.1)[b]	22.31	(19.3)[b]	28.56	(20.2)[b]	103.20	(29.6)[b]	99.69	(24.4)[b]	174.72	(31.7)[b]	192.50	(30.8)[b]

[a] Provisional.   [b] Percentage of total engineering exports.

Sources: Compiled from India, Ministry of Commerce, *Monthly Statistics of the Foreign Trade of India* and EEPC, *Handbook of Export Statistics.*

Appendix 5   Indian Exports to Iran, Iraq, Kuwait, Libya, Oman, Qatar, Saudi Arabia, UAE: Selected Years 1966–7 to 1977–8 (Rs. crore)

	1966–7		1970–1		1972–3		1974–5		1975–6		1976–7		1977–8	
	Amount	%	Amount	%	Amount	%	Amount	%	Amount	%	Amount	%	Amount	%
(i) Total	32.73	(100.00)	81.45	(100.00)	80.08	(100.00)	439.86	(100.00)	543.11	(100.00)	602.71	(100.00)	509.43	(100.00)
(ii) of which, engineering goods	5.81	(17.75)	22.31	(27.39)	28.56	(35.66)	103.20	(23.46)	99.69	(18.35)	174.72	(28.99)	192.50	(37.79)

Sources: As Appendix 4 above.

Appendix 6 Indian Engineering Exports by Commodity: Performance and Targets as at February 1979 (f.o.b., Rs. crore)

Item	Performance		Target		
	1976–7	1977–8[a]	1978–9	1979–80	1980–1
A. CAPITAL GOODS					
1. *Industrial Plant and Machinery:*	*43.19*	*45.00*	*66.00*	*85.00*	*110.00*
(a) Textile & Jute	15.11	9.50	12.00	18.00	25.00
(b) Sugar	2.46	2.50	12.00	13.00	15.00
(c) Cement	0.45	0.25	1.00	2.50	3.50
(d) Food Processing	4.14	6.00	6.00	8.00	9.50
(e) Others (incl. Excavators, Tractors, Coke Oven Plant, etc.)	21.03	26.75	35.00	43.50	57.00
2. Elec. Power Machinery & Switchgear	15.60	25.00	40.00	42.00	45.00
3. Transmission Line Towers	8.98	20.00	25.00	25.00	25.00
4. *Steel Structurals Fabricated:*	*18.77*	*31.00*	*35.00*	*38.00*	*42.00*
(a) Boilers incl. Pressure Vessels	1.92	7.50	8.00	8.00	9.00
(b) Cranes & Lifts	2.72	4.50	5.00	6.00	7.00
(c) Other Structurals	14.13	19.00	22.00	24.00	26.00
5. Wires & Cables	23.82	23.00	28.00	30.00	32.00
6. Wagons & Coaches	11.29	8.00	10.00	20.00	25.00
7. Coastal Vessels & Ships	6.18	8.00	10.00	13.00	15.00
8. Complete Vehicles	31.31	37.00	40.00	44.00	46.00
9. Machine Tools	16.93	18.00	21.00	23.00	25.00
SUB-TOTAL OF 'A'	176.07	215.00	275.00	320.00	365.00
B. PRIMARILY STEEL & PIG IRON BASED ITEMS					
1. Steel Pipes & Tubes	58.69	46.00	60.00	70.00	95.00
2. Bright Bars	9.12	8.00	8.00	12.00	13.00
3. Ferrous Hollow-ware	6.88	10.00	10.00	11.00	12.00
4. *Mild Steel Wire Products:*	*15.35*	*16.00*	*20.00*	*25.00*	*30.00*
(a) Electrodes	1.80	1.50	2.00	3.00	6.00
(b) Wire Nails, Nettings, Barbed Wires, etc.	13.55	14.50	18.00	22.00	24.00
5. *Industrial Fasteners:*	*11.86*	*16.50*	*18.00*	*21.00*	*25.00*
(a) Bolts, Nuts, Rivets & Washers	8.74	12.00	12.00	12.50	13.00
(b) Wood Screws	2.24	2.50	3.00	3.50	5.25
(c) Railway Track	0.88	2.00	3.00	5.00	6.75

Appendix 6—cont'd.

Item	Performance		Target		
	1976–7	1977–8[a]	1978–9	1979–80	1980–1
6. High Carbon Wire Products (Wire Ropes)	6.75	8.00	10.00	13.00	15.00
7. Sanitary Castings	22.97	25.00	25.00	28.00	33.00
8. Industrial Castings	2.13	2.50	2.50	5.00	10.00
9. Forgings	0.82	1.00	2.50	5.00	8.00
10. *Steel Products not otherwise specified:*	*17.39*	*22.00*	*24.00*	*30.00*	*34.00*
(a) Steel Furniture	4.31	4.75	5.00	6.25	7.00
(b) Builders' Hardware & Locks	4.35	6.00	6.50	7.00	8.00
(c) Stainless Steel Utensils & Cutlery	1.94	3.00	3.00	4.50	5.00
(d) Sanitary & Water Fittings	3.01	3.50	4.00	5.00	5.50
(e) Agricultural Implements & Machinery	3.34	3.00	3.50	5.00	6.00
(f) Razor Blades	0.44	1.75	2.00	2.25	2.50
SUB-TOTAL OF 'B'	151.96	155.00	180.00	220.00	275.00
C. NON-FERROUS PRODUCTS					
1. Aluminium Products	24.44	15.50	16.00	20.00	25.00
2. EPNS Ware	7.05	5.00	8.00	10.00	12.00
3. Non-ferrous Products (other than aluminium)	4.17	4.50	6.00	5.00	8.00
SUB-TOTAL OF 'C'	35.66	25.00	30.00	35.00	45.00
D. CONSUMER DURABLES					
1. Auto Parts	23.31	29.00	30.00	35.00	40.00
2. *Bicycles & Parts:*	*21.82*	*30.00*	*31.00*	*33.00*	*35.00*
(a) Complete	6.24	8.00	8.00	8.50	9.00
(b) Parts	15.58	22.00	23.00	24.50	26.00
3. Hand, Small & Cutting Tools including Abrasives	29.73	32.00	33.00	36.00	40.00
4. *Diesel Engines & Compressors:*	*35.71*	*40.50*	*42.00*	*45.00*	*50.00*
(a) Diesel Engines & Parts	33.64	38.00	39.00	41.00	43.00
(b) Air compressors	2.07	2.50	3.00	5.00	7.00
5. Mechanical Pumps	5.95	7.50	8.00	9.50	11.00
6. Heating & Cooling Equipment	3.41	3.50	4.50	5.00	6.00

Appendix 6—cont'd.

Item	Performance		Target		
	1976–7	1977–8[a]	1978–9	1979–80	1980–1
7. Elec. Fans & Parts	11.14	10.00	12.00	14.00	15.00
8. *Electronics:*	12.69	24.00	26.00	30.00	40.00
(a) Data Processing Machines	2.35	2.00	2.00	3.00	4.00
(b) Radios, Electronics Equipment and Parts	7.31	17.00	18.00	20.00	27.50
(c) PA Equipment	2.13	2.50	3.00	3.25	4.00
(d) Telephone & Teleprinters	0.90	2.50	3.00	3.75	4.50
9. *Batteries:*	10.42	13.00	14.50	16.00	17.00
(a) Dry Batteries	1.89	3.00	3.50	3.75	4.00
(b) Storage Batteries	8.53	10.00	11.00	12.25	13.00
10. Sewing Machines ⎫ 11. Knitting Machines ⎭	1.75	2.00	2.50	3.00	4.00
12. *Electric Manufactures not otherwise specified:*	13.59	11.50	14.00	19.00	23.00
(a) Electric Accessories & Appliances	9.49	7.00	9.00	13.00	14.00
(b) Electric Lamps	2.72	3.00	3.50	4.00	6.00
(c) Electric Products, Others	1.38	1.50	1.50	2.00	3.00
13. *Misc. Manufactured Articles:*	18.44	37.00	18.50	29.50	34.00
(a) Scientific & Surgical Instruments	3.22	4.00	4.00	9.00	10.00
(b) Oil Lamps	3.25	4.00	4.00	5.00	6.00
(c) Fire Arms of Sports	0.92	0.25	0.50	1.00	2.00
(d) Ball & Roller Bearings	0.82	1.25	1.50	2.50	3.00
(e) Umbrellas & Fittings	0.60	1.00	1.00	2.00	2.50
(f) Others	9.63	16.50	7.50	10.00	10.50
SUB-TOTAL OF 'D'	187.99	230.00	235.00	275.00	315.00
GRAND TOTAL OF (A+B+C+D)	551.68	625.00	720.00	850.00	1,000.00

[a] Estimated.

Source: EEPC, *Handbook of Export Statistics.*

Appendix 7   Indian Engineering Exports by Destination: Performance and Targets as at February 1979 (f.o.b., Rs. crore)

Region	Country	Performance		Target		
		1976–7	1977–8[a]	1978–9	1979–80	1980–1
South East Asia	Bangladesh	26.15	17.50	20.00	22.00	25.00
	Indonesia	13.20	15.50	16.00	18.00	19.00
	Malaysia	10.87	14.00	14.00	16.50	19.00
	Singapore	12.72	12.00	14.00	16.00	19.00
	Sri Lanka	15.75	19.50	21.00	23.00	25.00
	Thailand	9.16	11.00	12.00	13.00	16.00
		117.17 (21.23) (%)	120.00 (19.20) (%)	140.00	175.00	215.00
Middle East	Iran	28.45	38.00	40.00	40.00	41.00
	Iraq	19.14	25.00	35.00	38.00	41.00
	Kuwait	38.20	39.00	40.00	40.00	42.00
	Oman	8.50	9.00	10.00	11.00	12.00
	Qatar	4.54	9.50	10.00	11.00	12.00
	Saudi Arabia	25.43	35.00	37.00	39.00	42.00
	UAE	46.39	38.00	39.00	40.00	41.00
		198.65 (36.01)	223.00 (35.68)	245.00	260.00	280.00
Africa	Egypt	11.26	19.00	21.00	25.00	30.00
	Kenya	7.51	11.00	12.50	14.00	18.00
	Libya	4.06	20.00	28.00	38.00	45.00
	Nigeria	16.68	16.50	17.50	18.50	21.00
	Tanzania	17.17	21.00	21.50	25.00	28.50
		79.28 (14.37)	112.00 (17.92)	130.00	163.00	200.00
Europe	Germany, FR	18.16	23.40	26.50	30.00	34.00
	UK	16.98	21.00	25.00	29.00	30.00
	USSR	27.37	29.75	33.00	40.00	44.00
		108.58 (19.68)	115.00 (18.40)	135.00	165.00	195.00
America	USA	27.40	35.00	45.00	55.00	68.00
		36.45 (6.61)	43.00 (6.88)	55.00	70.00	90.00
Australasia etc.	Australia	5.60	8.00	9.00	9.50	11.00
		11.55 (2.09)	12.00 (1.92)	15.00	17.00	20.00
Total		551.68 (100)	625.00 (100)	720.00	850.00	1000.00

a Estimated.   *Source:* Compiled from EEPC, *Handbook of Export Statistics.*

Appendix 8 Volume Indices of Selected Indian Exports (1968–9=100)

	1970–1	1973–4	1974–5	1975–6	1976–7	1977–8
Non-ferrous metals	72	72	295	630	561	282
Iron and steel	78	42	36	54	173	139
Manufactures of metals	134	153	176	200	302	375
Machinery and transport eqpt	166	188	386	325	373	397
Misc. manufactured articles	151	283	341	410	620	633
General	106	125	133	147	174	168

Source: Compiled from Reserve Bank of India, *Report on Currency and Finance,* vol. 2: *Statistical Statements 1978–79* (Bombay), p. 132, (citing as its source Director General, Dept of Commercial Intelligence and Statistics, Govt of India).

Appendix 9 Public and Private Sector Expenditure on Construction[a] in Eight Middle Eastern Countries 1977 and 1978 ($ mn)

Country	1977	1978	% change over 1977
Iran	5305	3873	− 27
Iraq	2750	3355	+ 22
Kuwait	1020	1071	+ 5
Libya	1433	1247	− 13
Oman	483	382	− 21
Qatar	461	309	− 33
Saudi Arabia	10390	11845	+ 14
UAE	2279	1235	− 37

[a] 'Plantecon define "construction expenditure" as containing "bricks and mortar" only, i.e. abstracting mechanical, (petro) chemical, electrical, etc., installations.'

Source: Compiled from *Financial Times,* 26 June 1979, citing Plantecon Overseas (Research).

Appendix 10 Labour Disputes in India, Republic of Korea, Singapore, and the United Kingdom 1973–8 (thousand)

Year	India Man-days lost (a)	India Emplo-yees (b)	Republic of Korea Man-days lost (c)	Republic of Korea Emplo-yees (d)	Singapore Man-days lost	Singapore Emplo-yees (e) (f)	United Kingdom Man-days lost (g)	United Kingdom Emplo-yees (f) (h)
1973	20211	17625	0	5568	2	n.a.	7196	23906
1974	37385	18047	17	6002	5	803	14728	24024
1975	21829	18405	14	6403	5	816	6011	23929
1976	12694	18860	17	6954	3	851	3284	23764
1977	24698	19332	8	7524	1	884	10142	23882*
1978	21140*	19917	13	8311	0	941	9404	23953*

Man-days lost = working days lost in industrial disputes less working day lost in Agriculture, Forestry, and Fishing.

Employees = employment in non-agricultural sectors.

* provisional.

n.a. Not available.

(a) Disputes involving 10 or more workers; excluding political strikes.
(b) Including working proprietors.
(c) Excluding workers indirectly affected.
(d) Persons aged 14 years and over.
(e) Persons aged 10 years and over.
(f) June of each year.
(g) Excluding disputes not connected with terms of employment or conditions of labour. Disputes involving less than 10 workers or lasting less than 1 day are not included unless a loss of more than 100 working days is involved.
(h) Civilian labour force employed (official estimates).

Sources: Compiled from ILO, Year Book of Labour Statistics 1979, Tables 5 and 25, and ILO, Bulletin of Labour Statistics, 3rd and 4th Quarters 1980, Table 2.

Appendix 11 British Imports from India: Selected Years 1947–78 (c.i.f., £ mn)

	SITC	1947	1950	1955	1960	1965	1970	1975	1976	1977	1978
Tea	074.1	29.23	34.71	75.50	63.52	51.52	37.15	44.03	58.46	113.29	40.26
Tobacco and Manufactures	12	3.09	7.86	7.16	9.19	8.58	10.57	22.43	25.61	35.16	36.03
Leather and Manufactures	61	11.81	11.15	12.62	12.92	8.96	8.41	16.47	26.59	28.15	25.04
Unwrought Silver	681.11	—	—	—	—	—	0	58.83	65.60	13.31	31.21
Clothing	84	0.01	0.06	0.15	0.18	0.34	1.23	10.88	28.28	29.46	27.16
Cotton Fabrics (woven)	652	0.19	4.57	6.76	13.00	10.05	7.07	7.97	29.89	35.20	32.29
Total UK Imports from India		94.74	98.35	158.95	148.46	128.34	105.27	237.14	355.07	384.14	322.06
Products as % of total											
Tea		30.85	35.29	47.49	42.78	40.14	35.29	18.56	16.46	29.49	12.50
Tobacco and Manufactures		3.26	7.99	4.50	6.19	6.68	10.04	9.45	7.21	9.15	11.18
Leather and Manufactures		12.47	11.34	7.93	8.70	6.98	7.98	6.94	7.48	7.32	7.77
Unwrought Silver		—	—	—	—	—	—	24.80	18.47	3.46	9.69
Clothing		0.01	0.06	0.09	0.12	0.26	1.16	4.58	7.96	7.66	8.43
Cotton Fabrics (woven)		0.20	4.65	4.25	8.75	7.83	6.71	3.36	8.41	9.16	10.02

Source: Compiled from Great Britain, Dept of Trade, *Overseas Trade Statistics of the United Kingdom.*

Appendix 12　British Exports to India: Selected Years 1947–78
(f.o.b., £ mn)

	SITC	1947	1950	1960	1970	1975	1976	1977	1978
Chemical Elements and Compounds	51	3.72	2.66	5.67	2.61	3.39	7.21	9.65	9.43
Diamonds	667.2	n.a.	n.a.	n.a.	2.21	16.19	34.93	70.90	106.96
Iron and Steel	67	5.16	6.08	15.43	9.51	17.84	30.04	22.61	36.34
Non-ferrous Metals	68	5.47	2.61	3.75	2.67	4.23	6.28	8.05	8.08
Non-electric Machinery	71	29.99	36.00	43.66	18.48	42.60	56.46	61.84	73.08
Electrical Machinery and Parts	72	6.77	6.64	14.96	7.41	17.64	15.11	17.86	12.23
Transport Equipment	73	12.32	18.30	29.83	8.18	30.52	17.32	19.66	23.63
Total Exports to India		92.10	97.23	151.52	72.93	164.54	206.92	278.10	348.64
Products as % of total:									
Chemical Elements and Compounds		4.04	2.74	3.74	3.58	2.06	3.48	3.47	2.70
Diamonds		n.a.	n.a.	n.a.	3.03	9.84	16.88	25.49	30.68
Iron and Steel		5.60	6.25	10.18	13.04	10.84	14.52	8.13	10.42
Non-ferrous Metals		5.94	2.68	2.47	3.66	2.57	3.03	2.89	2.32
Non-electric Machinery		32.56	37.03	28.81	25.34	25.89	27.29	22.24	20.96
Electrical Machinery and Parts		7.35	6.83	9.87	10.16	10.72	7.30	6.42	3.51
Transport Equipment		13.38	18.82	19.69	11.22	18.55	8.37	7.07	6.78

Source: As Appendix 11 above.

Appendix 13　Indo-British Trade Balance: Selected Years 1948–78
(£ mn)

	1948	1950	1955	1960	1965	1970	1971
UK exports[a] (f.o.b.)	96.6	97.2	130.1	151.3	116.4	72.9	138.3
UK imports[a] (c.i.f.)	96.3	98.3	159.0	148.5	128.3	105.3	111.2
Balance of trade	+0.3	—1.1	—28.9	+2.8	—11.9	—32.4	+27.1

	1972	1973	1974	1975	1976	1977	1978
UK exports[a] (f.o.b.)	140.9	134.8	128.8	165.6	208.5	277.9	348.6
UK imports[a] (c.i.f.)	112.2	148.3	202.5	235.5	355.8	387.4	322.1
Balance of trade	+28.7	—13.5	—73.7	—69.9	—147.3	—10.5	+26.5

[a] Not including diamonds before 1960.

Source : Compiled from Great Britain, Central Statistical Office, *Annual Abstract of Statistics*.

Appendix 14 Origin of Indian Imports 1975–6 and 1976–7
(Rs. crore)

Country	1975–6	%	1976–7	%
USA	1285.22	24.41	1055.53	21.06
Iran	459.88	8.73	507.87	10.13
Saudi Arabia	290.13	5.51	331.98	6.62
UK	284.00	5.39	321.29	6.41
USSR	309.78	5.88	307.24	6.13
FRG	369.96	7.03	305.64	6.10
Japan	361.18	6.86	297.05	5.93
Iraq	247.77	4.71	280.17	5.59
Australia	101.67	1.93	249.57	4.98
France	196.53	3.73	140.21	2.80
Canada	232.01	4.41	129.40	2.58
UAE	81.59	1.55	84.53	1.69
Kuwait	62.64	1.19	77.29	1.54
Netherlands	63.82	1.21	65.22	1.30
Italy	84.83	1.61	57.44	1.15
Belgium	86.49	1.64	57.10	1.14
Switzerland	55.41	1.05	49.04	0.98
Tanzania	24.03	0.46	47.66	0.95
Zaire	11.52	0.22	44.70	0.89
Zambia	11.35	0.22	40.77	0.81
Poland	81.04	1.54	37.99	0.76
Sweden	68.47	1.30	35.75	0.71
Czechoslovakia	53.01	1.00	34.13	0.68
Malaysia	14.58	0.28	33.93	0.68
Nepal	33.15	0.63	33.49	0.67
GDR	36.59	0.69	30.14	0.60
Romania	38.35	0.73	28.33	0.57
Afghanistan	12.54	0.24	26.84	0.54
Yugoslavia	11.00	0.21	23.87	0.48
Brazil	7.06	0.13	21.65	0.43
Egypt	18.99	0.36	21.14	0.42
Austria	7.98	0.15	20.90	0.42
Sudan	3.64	0.07	19.04	0.38
Mexico	14.47	0.27	15.18	0.30
Hungary	25.10	0.48	14.77	0.29
All other countries	629.00	11.95	164.18	3.28
Total	5264.78	100.00	5011.03	100.00

Source: Compiled from India, Cabinet Secretariat, *Monthly Abstract of Statistics*, March 1979.

Appendix 15   Aid to India from Main DAC Donors and Multilateral Agencies 1969–77 (US\$ mn)

	1969	1970	1971	1972	1973	1974	1975	1976	1977[a],[b]
Official Development Assistance (ODA), Net									
Total DAC Bilateral of which:[c]	752.9	752.3	848.0	445.4	456.7	602.2	819.5	725.2	478.0
United Kingdom	47.6 (6.3)	86.7 (11.5)	126.0 (14.9)	110.6 (24.8)	88.9 (19.5)	141.7 (23.5)	113.8 (13.9)	163.9 (22.6)	154.4 (32.5)
USA	498.0 (66.1)	418.0 (55.6)	454.0 (53.5)	104.0 (23.3)	84.0 (18.4)	91.0 (15.1)	225.0 (27.5)	135.0 (18.6)	42.8 (9.0)
Japan	33.9 (4.5)	32.7 (4.3)	33.5 (4.0)	26.7 (6.0)	69.0 (15.1)	64.8 (10.8)	46.6 (5.7)	79.4 (10.9)	28.6 (6.0)
Germany	58.1 (7.7)	50.3 (6.7)	54.9 (6.5)	60.2 (13.5)	59.4 (13.0)	59.8 (9.9)	92.6 (11.3)	90.6 (12.5)	−0.2 (—)
Canada	69.8 (9.3)	105.8 (14.1)	104.8 (12.4)	70.4 (15.8)	54.8 (12.0)	112.6 (18.7)	109.3 (13.3)	66.9 (9.2)	41.1 (8.7)
Total Multilateral of which:[d]	152.6	72.6	154.8	168.6	322.8	520.5	685.2	595.8	407.7
International Development Association	135.7 (88.9)	45.7 (62.9)	115.3 (74.5)	112.6 (66.8)	276.2 (85.6)	421.3 (80.9)	456.3 (66.6)	526.0 (88.3)	324.7 (79.6)
OPEC donors Total Net ODA	n.a.	n.a.	n.a.	n.a.	n.a.	235.0	203.7	499.5	311.5

[a] Fiscal year, all others calendar years.

[b] Estimate.

[c] Figures in parentheses show percentage of total bilateral aid from DAC (Development Assistance Committee of OECD) countries.

[d] Figures in parentheses show percentage of total aid from multilateral agencies.

Source: Compiled from OECD, *Geographical Distribution of Financial Flows to Developing Countries.*

Appendix 16 British Aid to India 1967–77 (£ mn)

	1967	1968	1969	1970	1971	1972	1973	1974	1975	1976	1977
Gross Official Development Assistance (ODA)	37.5	40.1	34.0	44.8	62.1	55.8	49.4	75.4	68.1	109.3	79.8
of which (%):											
Project aid	n.a.	2.0	6.6	3.2	17.8	27.2	47.9	27.2	26.6	31.3	16.8
Non-project aid	n.a.	96.3	90.8	94.9	80.4	70.7	49.9	71.2	71.1	67.3	80.4
Technical co-operation	1.9	1.7	2.6	1.9	1.8	2.1	2.2	1.5	2.3	1.4	2.8
Net ODA[a]	26.5	27.2	19.8	36.1	51.8	44.3	36.3	60.6	51.2	90.7	61.3
Net transfer[b]	17.9	19.0	12.2	29.2	42.5	33.9	26.6	51.6	43.0	83.2	54.4
UK aid to India os percentage of total UK aid											
Bilateral, gross	20.6	21.8	19.1	23.1	25.6	25.0	22.3	28.3	22.3	29.0	20.6
Net ODA	17.2	17.6	13.5	21.7	25.3	23.0	20.0	26.9	19.6	27.5	18.7
Net transfer	14.0	14.9	10.0	20.5	24.6	21.0	17.8	28.0	19.5	28.8	18.9

[a] Net ODA = aid payments minus amortization of previous aid payments.

[b] Net transfer = aid payments minus interest and amortization.

Source: Compiled from Great Britain, Ministry of Overseas Development, *British Aid Statistics.*

Appendix 17   Underspending of British Aid to India 1968–9 to 1977–8
(£ mn)

Year	Total expenditure	Amount by which short of budget
1968–69	27.061	1.611
1969–70	33.990	5.303
1970–71	42.370	3.025
1971–72	60.434	7.011
1972–73	71.410	3.806
1973–74	77.229	8.265
1974–75	60.509	2.073
1975–76	79.245	4.450
1976–77	95.710	3.800
1977–78	103.039	17.472

Note: These figures do not include technical co-operation.
Source: House of Commons Debates (Hansard), vol. 960, Written Answers, 16 Jan. 1979, col. 706.

Appendix 18   British Investment in India 1972–6[a]

	1972	1973	1974	1975	1976
Investment: Annual flow (£ mn)	4.2	10.2	17.1	23.3	17.3
Stock (end year, £ mn)	279.0	274.8	275.3	298.6	315.9
Annual flow (% total to LDCs)	4.9	4.2	7.0	7.2	3.5
Stock (% total in LDCs)	14.5	13.6	12.7	12.0	10.7
Earnings (£ mn)	25.6	26.5	35.5	33.6	53.9
Earnings (%)	9.2	9.2	11.6	10.2	15.5
Earnings (% return on investment in all LDCs)	12.9	17.8	19.3	18.9	23.3

Sectoral shares 1974 (%)

Food, drink and tobacco	19.6	Paper, printing, publishing	1.5
Chemicals	14.6	Other manufacturing net	6.9
Metal manufactures	3.1	*Total manufacturing*	69.3
Mechanical and instrument		Distributive trades	3.3
engineering	4.0	Agriculture, forestry, fishing	17.8
Electrical engineering	14.8	Other	9.6
Textiles, leather, clothing,			
footwear	4.8		

a Book values of British investment, excluding oil, banking, and insurance.
Sources: Compiled from *Business Monitor M4,* 1974 Supplement, Census of Overseas Assets 1974; and *Trade and Industry,* 9 June 1978.

Appendix 19   *Indo-British Industrial Collaboration Agreements 1970–7*

Year	Technical collaboration only		Technical collaboration with equity participation		Total	
	Engineering	Total	Engineering	Total	Engineering	Total
1970	27	35	3	4	30	39
1971	25	45	6	10	41	55
1972	30	30	—	8	30	38
1973	38	47	5	5	43	52
1974	36	53	—	6	36	59
1975	34	52	2	2	36	54
1976	41	50	4	4	45	54
1977 (Jan.-Sept.)	25	27	3	6	28	33
1977 (whole year)	n.a.	50	n.a.	9	n.a.	59

Source: Compiled from data supplied by Association of Indian Engineering Industry.

Appendix 20   Contracts Secured by Indian Companies in Iraq as at November 1979

Project	Company	Client	Value (US$ mn)	Date of award	Date of completion
3 bridges on Baghdad-Hussaiba railway	Asia Foundations & Constructions Pvt. Ltd, Bombay (AFCONS)	State Contracting Company for Construction (SCCC)	11.1	29.1.79	May 1981
Fender piles for oil jetty, Mufiah	AFCONS	State Organization for Oil Projects (SOOP)	0.75	4.12.78	Aug. 1979
Sewerage scheme, Najaf-Kufa	Bridge & Roof, Calcutta	State Construction Company for Water & Sewerage Projects (SCCWASP)	4.8	1.1.78	1,000 days from 1.1.78
Trunk sewer, Kerbala	Bridge & Roof, Calcutta	SCCWASP	6.0	30.6.79	June 1981
Water sewerage network, Sulaimaniya	Continental Construction Co., New Delhi	SCCWASP	27.0	7.10.79	Sept. 1980
Sewerage scheme, Amara	Continental Construction Co., New Delhi	SCCWASP	7.8	15.3.78	
Sewerage scheme, Nassiriya	Continental Construction Co., New Delhi	SCCWASP	27.6	14.12.78	June 1981
Laying of gas pipelines (various areas)	Dodsals	SOOP	22.0		
Expansion, Baghdad Radio & Colour TV Centre	Engineering Projects (India) Ltd, New Delhi (EPI)	Mitsubishi Corporation, Tokyo, for Ministry of Information, Iraq	14.4	Oct. 1978	Dec. 1978
Northern Grain Silos, Sinjar, Shirkat, Talafar	EPI	State Organization for Buildings (SOB) and State Grain Organization	47.0	6.4.78	Dec. 1980
Central Grain Silos, Khanakin, Baquba, Tuz	EPI	SOB and State Grain Organization	45.0	9.10.78	Aug. 1981

Appendix 20—cont'd.

Project	Company	Client	Value (US$ mn)	Date of award	Date of completion
Water Research Centre [irrigation research], Baghdad	EPI	Ministry of Irrigation	16.5	3.2.79	Aug. 1981
Council of Ministers Building, Baghdad	EPI	SOB	35.7	15.5.79	Oct. 1981
Bridge, Daqooqchai	Hindustan Construction Co. Ltd, Bombay	State Organization for Roads & Bridges (SORB)	7.5	5.8.79	Feb. 1981
429 culverts on Akashat-al-Qaim railway	Indian Road Construction Corporation Ltd (IRCC)	SCCC	16.2	6.3.79	Sept. 1980
Bridge, Jalawala	IRCC	SORB	9.6	2.5.78	Nov. 1980
Trunk sewer, Baghdad	Jaiprakash Associates, New Delhi	SCCWASP	13.3	16.9.79	May 1983
2 flyovers on Airport Road, Baghdad	National Buildings Construction Corporation Ltd (NBCC)	Amanat al-Asima	6.0	18.1.79	Feb. 1981
Baghdad University complex	NBCC	SCCC	6.0	7.10.78	Apr. 1981
1,120 pre-fabricated housing units, Diwaniya	Punjab Chemi Plants, Chandigarh	State Establishment for Industrial Housing	29.1	19.5.79	Oct. 1981
Bridge, Khidr	Shah Construction, Bombay	SORB	5.1	16.5.78	May 1980
Bridge, Hillah	Shah Construction, Bombay	SORB	2.1	24.5.78	May 1980
1,700 pre-fabricated housing units, Baghdad	Som Dutt (Builders), New Delhi	SOOP	51.0	28.4.79	Oct. 1981
4 bridges on Kirkuk-Mosul road	UP State Bridge Corporation	SORB	3.9	15.4.79	June 1981
Supply & erection of 3 propane tanks, Baghdad	Vijay Tanks & Vessels, Madras	SOOP	5.0	June 1979	Dec. 1980

Source: Indian Embassy Baghdad.

*Appendix 21   Contracts and Joint Ventures Secured by Indian Companies
in Kuwait as at November 1979*

A. CONTRACTS

Auto and General Manufacturing Company. A contract for erection, commissioning, and running of a galvanizing plant for Kuwait Prefabricating and Building Co., valued at Rs. 1.79 mn (in progress).

Braithwaite & Co. Contract for supply and erection of 12 pressed steel tanks for the Ministry of Electricity & Water, valued at Rs. 1.6 mn (in progress).

Corrosion Control Services

(a) Contract for industrial X-ray inspection on two power projects, valued at Rs. 7.5 mn (completed).
(b) Sub-contract for coating and wrapping underground steel pipes, valued at Rs. 3.3 mn (completed).

Engineering Projects India Ltd

(a) Turnkey contract for the construction of a complete township—the Ardiya Housing Project—valued at Rs. 230 crore (in progress).
(b) Sub-contract for the fabrication and erection of structural steel for the new Kuwait International Airport Terminal, valued at Rs. 3 crore (completed).
(c) Contract for Sief Palace extension, valued at Rs. 30 crore (in progress).
(d) Contract for the construction of 35th Brigade camp, valued at Rs. 75 crore (in progress).
(e) Contract for the construction of temporary housing units (at the Ardiya Housing Project) valued at Rs. 6 crore (in progress).

Punj Brothers Ltd. Contract for ducting and insulation work at Doha Power Station, valued at Rs. 6 mn (completed).

Punjab Chemi Plants Ltd. Two sub-contracts for pipe laying and building of mosques, schools, and a shopping centre, worth about Rs. 3 crore each (in progress).

Stup Consultants

(a) A continuing consultancy contract with the National Industries Company of Kuwait for consultancy in complex structures of prestressed concrete.
(b) Sub-contract valued at Rs. 1.2 mn to prepare tender documents and drawings for a 16,000 sq. metre maintenance hangar for Boeing 747 aircraft of Kuwait Airways Corporation (in progress).

Tata Consulting Engineers Ltd. Contract for erection of turbines at Shuwaikh Power Station, valued at Rs. 8.8 mn (completed).

Telecommunications Consultants India Ltd

(a) Contract for repair, rehabilitation, and refurbishing of 200 pairs of cables from the Ministry of Communications, valued at Rs. 426,000 (completed).

Appendix 21—cont'd.

(b) Sub-contract for laying of 60 km of junction cables, valued at Rs. 3 mn (in progress).

(c) Contract for de-loading of telephone lines, valued at Rs. 99,000.

Vijay Tanks and Vessels Pvt. Ltd

(a) Contract for design, supply, and erection of 6 petroleum storage tanks with complete civil works for Kuwait Aviation Fuelling Co., valued at Rs. 3.45 mn (completed).

(b) Contract for replacement of 3 crude oil storage tanks with connected civil, electrical, and instrumentation work for Kuwait Oil Co. (KOC) valued at Rs. 7.66 mn (in progress).

Western India Erectors Ltd

(a) Two contracts from Arabian Oil Co. for overhauling gas tanks, valued at Rs. 0.46 crore (completed).

(b) Contract for shifting gas tanks, valued at Rs. 195,000 (completed).

(c) Sub-contract for erection of four 150 MW boilers for Doha Power Station, valued at Rs. 3 crore (completed).

(d) Sub-contract for the erection of electrical and instrumentation work for the KOC's gas project, valued at Rs. 0.24 crore (completed).

Source: Indian Embassy, Kuwait.

B. JOINT VENTURES

Indo-Burmah Petroleum Co. Ltd-Balmer Lawrie of India have a joint venture with Abdul Hashim Gharabally and have set up a workshop for repair of electric motors, transformers, switchgear, etc. (continuing).

Lightcraft Corporation of Bombay has a joint-venture collaboration with Yousif Khalid al-Adasani Est. for manufacture of PVC plastic fittings for electric conduits, water pipes, etc. The Indian company is to provide technical know-how for a fixed amount of Rs. 90,000 a year and also a share of 24.5 per cent in the profits of the company (continuing).

Mohd Nasser al-Sayer Est. has a bottling franchise from Parle Bottling Co. of Bombay for bottling and marketing Limca and Maza (Gold Spot) soft drinks (continuing).

The State Bank of India has signed an agreement with Ateeqy Trading Enterprises for a joint-venture foreign exchange company (operations started in the autumn of 1979).

Yousuf al-Ghanim & Sons has an arrangement with Blue Star Engineering of Bombay for assembly of refrigerated water coolers (continuing).

Source: Indian Embassy, Kuwait.

Appendix 22   Contracts Secured by Indian Companies in Libya
as at September 1979

Project	Company	Value (US$ mn)	Remarks
Extension of Tripoli West Power Station	Bharat Heavy Electricals Ltd. New Delhi	115	Completion by 1980
Dam at Wadi Ghan	Continental Construction Pvt. Ltd, Delhi	80	Completion by 1980
Consultancy, Misurata Steel Plant	Dastur Engineering Co., Calcutta	20	Under execution
Management and operations contract of Homs II cement plant	Development Consultants Pvt. Ltd, Calcutta	10	Work started in Sept. 1979
Laying of pipelines	Dodsals Pvt. Ltd, Bombay	25	Completed
Construction of 28 schools in Nalut-Garian area	Hindustan Steel Works Construction Ltd, Calcutta (HSC)	30	Work started in Sept. 1979
Koranic School & Training Centre, Tripoli	HSC	18	Work due to start late 1979
Schools in Beida-Tobruk area	HSC	15	Work due to start late 1979
Agricultural roads at Zleitan	Indian Road Construction Corporation Ltd, New Delhi	16	Completion by 1979 end
Hotels at Sabrata and Cyrene	Indian Tobacco Co. Ltd—National Buildings Construction Corporation Ltd, New Delhi (NBCC)	60	Work due to start late 1979
Airport at Ghat	International Airports Authority of India, New Delhi (IAAI)	45	Partly completed
Airport at Brak	IAAI	24	Completion by 1981
Terminal Building at Ghat airport	IAAI	4.5	Completion by 1981
Transmission lines over 1,000 km	Kamani Engineering Corporation, Bombay	85	6 different contracts

Appendix 22—cont'd.

Project	Company	Value (US$ mn)	Remarks
Hospital and 1,305 housing units at Ghat and Beniwalid	NBCC	100	Completion by 1979 end
Miscellaneous work at Ghat and Beniwalid	NBCC	2	Under execution
124 classrooms for 10 schools at Beniwalid	NBCC	10	Completion by 1981
Construction of dispensary, motel, and office at Beniwalid	NBCC	10	Work started in Sept. 1979
Orban township (first stage)	NBCC	45	Work due to start late 1979
Studies—Regional Industrial Development Studies	National Industrial Development Corporation, New Delhi		A 5-year industrial development plan for the period 1976–80, undertaken in 1975
Textile mill, Zanzaw	Star Trading Company, Bombay	14	Completed
9 oil storage tanks at Brak	Vijay Tanks & Vessels Pvt. Ltd, Bombay	2	Completion by 1981

Source: Indian Embassy, Tripoli.

Appendix 23   Contracts Secured by Indian Companies in Saudi Arabia as at May 1979

Bharat Heavy Electricals Ltd. Contract for electrification programme at Jizan.

Bombay Suburban Electric Supply Co. Contract for transmission line for Jizan project.

Corrosion Control Services (in conjunction with the Saudi NDT). Contract to inspect pipelines for Tamini & Fouad and for Petromin.

Dalal Consultants. Contract for housing in al-Jauf and Hail.

Deccan Industries. Contract to manage rubber rings plant for Saudi Amiantit.

Development Consultants Private Ltd (DCPL). Contract as consultants to Riyadh Electricity Corporation for contract taken in the name of DCPL's American associate, Kuljian Corporation.

Dredging Corporation of India. Contract to manage Yanbu Port.

Engineering Projects (India) Ltd (EPI). Contract as civil engineers to Bharat Heavy Electricals Ltd for Jizan project.

Oberoi Hotels. Contract to manage Dammam Hotel; and Dammam-Oberoi, under construction.

Saudi Ensas. Contract for air conditioning of Kanoo Building in Jeddah.

B.G. Shirke. Design consultancy for four-star hotel and highrise residential apartments in Riyadh; management of Siporex factory in Riyadh. Is consultant to The Gulf Contractor, which is the main contractor.

Som Dutt (Builders). Sub-contractor to EPI for Jizan project; sub-contractor to Omar K. al-Esayi for construction of an institute for mentally handicapped in Jeddah.

Vijay Tanks & Vessels (through EPI). Contract for 8 aviation fuel tanks in new Jeddah Airport (sub-contract to Petrola Engineering).

Voltas. Contract with al-Ernia Establishment for drilling of water wells.

Source: Indian Embassy, Jeddah.

Appendix 24   Contracts & Joint Ventures Secured by Indian Companies in the UAE as at September 1979

A. CONTRACTS

Indian company	Cost of project (UAE dirham)	UAE client	Item	Remarks
Balmer Lawrie & Co., New Delhi	18.5 mn	Abu Dhabi National Oil Co. (ADNOC)	Turnkey project for 14,000 tpd oil lubricants plant at Abu Dhabi	Contract signed 7 May 1978
Dastur Consultancy	No investment	A.W. Galadari, Dubai	Large landscaping job	Under construction
Engineering Projects (India) Ltd	6.8 mn	ADNOC	Sub-contract for civil works for refinery at Ruwais, Abu Dhabi	Contract signed 1 Nov. 1978
Engineers India Ltd	0.4 mn	ADNOC	Consultancy for multi-purpose pipeline at al-Ain	Contract initialled 26 June 1979
Gammon India Ltd, Bombay	Projects executed 2.25 mn	Gammon (Khansaheb) Ltd, Sharjah	Building Sharjah International Airport	Inaugurated 21 Apr. 1979
Gammon India Ltd	1.8 mn	Gammon (Khansaheb) Ltd, Sharjah	Sub-contract to Sumitomo Heavy Industries Ltd for mechanical erection of desalination plant at Jebel Ali, Dubai	Under construction
Green Fields, Poona	Executed order worth 2 mn	A.W. Galadari, Dubai	Large landscaping job	
Hyderabad Asbestos, Hyderabad	Total order: 15 mn	Crown Prince of Um-al-Quwein	Turnkey project for setting up asbestos sheet manufacturing plant	Under construction
B.G. Shirke, Poona	Executed orders worth 3.20 mn	Pan-Gulf Construction Co., Dubai	Houses for the Ruler of Dubai	Under construction

Source: Indian Embassy, Abu Dhabi.

Appendix 24—cont'd.

B. JOINT VENTURES

Indian company	Cost of project (UAE dirham)	UAE joint collaborator	Item	Remarks
al-Basti Mukta & Thapar Group, Bombay	Total investment: 6 mn Annual turnover: 20 mn	Dubai Salt & Chemicals Ltd, Ruler of Dubai	Salt factory, 14,000 tpy	Under construction
Alembic Chemical Works Ltd, Baroda	Investment: 12.5 mn	Arab Pharmaceutical Co. Ltd, Ajman	Manufacture of pharmaceuticals	
Ballarpur Industries Ltd, Bombay	Investment: 2.5 mn Projects executed: 600 mn	al-Basti Mukta Associates, Dubai	Importation of building & engineering materials	
Balmer Lawrie & Co., New Delhi	Investment: 10 mn	Caltex (Alkhalij) Ltd, Dubai	Container plant	Production started
Em-Tech International, Madras	Investment: 2 mn	Bin Turkiya & Mohan Mechanical Engineering Co., Dubai	Engineering & technological expertise	
Essar Construction Ltd, Delhi	Investment: 8 mn	A.W. Galadari, Dubai	Civil engineering & construction. Trading in building materials	Office set up in Dubai
Garment Plastics Pvt. Ltd, Bombay	Investment: 1.2 mn	Arabian Oil Auto Suppliers, Sharjah	Manufacturing PVC elect. conduit pipes	
R.M. Goculdas, Bombay	Capital: 2 mn Annual turnover: 12 mn	Cylinges Co. Ltd, Dubai	Producing pressure vessels	Production started in 1976
R.M. Goculdas, Bombay	Capital: 1 mn Annual turnover: 5 mn	Felcon Chemicals, Dubai	Sulphuric acid	Working at one-third capacity
Green Fields, Poona	Capital outlay: 0.5 mn	A.W. Galadari, Dubai	Agricultural landscaping unit	Under construction

Appendix 24: B—cont'd.

Indian company	Cost of project (UAE dirham)	UAE joint collaborator	Item	Remarks
N.N. Guja (P) Ltd, Bombay	Investment: 2.25 mn	Victory Navigation & Shipping, Sharjah	Setting up grinding factory	Production started
Khandelval Group, Bombay	Investment: 7 mn	Arabian Oasis Co., Dubai	Steel scaffolding	Functioning
Larsen & Toubro, Bombay	Investment: 25 mn	A.W. Galadari, Dubai	Turnkey project for a Crown Cork plant	Under process
Osnar Paints & Contracts Pvt. Ltd, Bombay	Investment: 2 mn	Mostfirm Engineering & Trading Enterprises, Dubai	Manufacture of paints	Under negotiation
Parle Products Manufacturing Co. Pvt. Ltd, Bombay		Union Beverages, Sharjah	Soft drinks	Production stage nearing completion
Pure Ice Cream Co. (1967) Ltd, Bombay	Investment: 4.2 mn	Pure Ice Cream Co. Ltd, Sharjah	Ice cream	Construction of the building started. Ice cream imported from India avaiable in market
Ramanad Sagar & Co., Bombay	Investment: 300,000	Oriental Film Agency, Dubai	Film procurement and distribution	Offices set up in India and Dubai
Sheoparshad Bhagwatparshad & Co., Calcutta	Investment: 2.5 mn Turnover: 5 mn	Pan-Gulf, Ruler of Dubai	Tea bags	Production started
Supreme Industries Ltd, Bombay	Capital: 2 mn	al-Lauz Enterprises, Dubai	Production of plastic goods	Government of India's sanction received
Tata, Bombay	Investment: 2.5 mn	Bukhtir Group, Sharjah	Electrostatic dust precipitator	Deal finalized
Usha Martin Black (Wire Ropes), New Delhi	Investment: 1 mn	Roodai Trading Co. Ltd, Dubai	Wire rope	Under negotiation

Source: Indian Embassy, Abu Dhabi.

Appendix 25   'Prospects for BHEL', Editorial Article in The Economic Times (New Delhi), 13 November 1978

There are disconcerting signs of anguish and demoralisation among design engineers and senior technical persons in Bharat Heavy Electricals Ltd. (BHEL) over the umbrella type of agreement proposed to be signed with Siemens. Significantly, this proposal was pushed through at a meeting of the board of directors of BHEL in early June this year soon after its chief Mr. S. V. S. Raghavan had been eased out and the memorandum of understanding was signed by the ministry of industry in September. Protagonists of this tie-up claim that the agreement would place at the disposal of BHEL the most modern product and system design and enable joint participation in research and development thereby providing BHEL with muscle power to crash into the highly competitive markets abroad by virtue of its superior technology. However, the validity of such claims is questioned in responsible quarters and not only in BHEL. The experience of BHEL itself is not very encouraging with previous agreements which had limited scope. The first agreement, which was signed with Siemens in April 1974 for high speed industrial turbines, was expected to provide BHEL with vital design information, but even manufacturing activity gained momentum only last year, and the expectation regarding design information remains largely unfulfilled. The existing operations are based only on manufacturing drawings and know-how. The second and third agreements were by-products of the emergency in 1975. These agreements provided for collaboration in the field of power electronics and thyristor devices. It was evident then and confirmed now that no in-depth study and cost-benefit assessment were made. Three years after the agreements progress in the design and manufacturing areas remains unsatisfactory. The Rs. 20-crore contract for Bokaro Steel Plant is perhaps an illustration that in these areas BHEL has essentially acted as a selling agent. The fourth agreement was even more questionable and again an offshoot of the emergency. This was signed in September 1976 with Kraft World Union (KWU), [i.e. Kraftwerk Union] a subsidiary of Siemens, for 200–1000 mw, turbosets. The development of high capacity turbosets had been originally assigned to the R and D division of BHEL, but the assignment was abruptly cancelled in January 1976. In certain aspects of this project for making higher capacity turbosets perhaps suitable technical collaboration was called for. But there was nothing to suggest that proper homework had been done and suitable alternatives considered before striking a deal with KWU. This deal had the effect of spelling frustration among the design engineers of BHEL. And tangible results are not fully in sight yet. Apart from the fact that this deal involves a complete change in technology, the fact remains that almost two years had elapsed before the project report itself became available. Reportedly the Centre is considering an investment of Rs. 50-crore for setting up an entirely new factory for the manufacture of KWU turbines. Meanwhile KWU has secured several firm orders for the import of turbosets, complete or in parts. Some gain this!

The latest umbrella type agreement which has sparked off a controversy, will tie-up BHEL to the Siemens' bandwagon for an indefinitely long period. Interested parties suggest that this tie-up would involve Siemens only in modernising stem [steam] turbines and generators of 200–1000 mw. range and certain other products aggregating a mere 37 per cent of BHEL's total turnover. This is an eye-wash. The scheme covers a wide range of products including transformers, switchgear, AC/DC motors, special purpose motors, hydro-generators and even turbines of capacity below 200 mw. and so on. The list covers more than 22 products, besides systems engineering. Nearly 70 per cent of BHEL's production will he linked to the fortunes and predilections of Siemens for at least a couple of decades if the Cabinet accorded its sanction to the proposed scheme. It is no secret that many developed countries have not taken kindly to India's entry in the field of sophisticated capital goods market including heavy electrical engineering. Their representatives in India have been carrying on whispering campaigns designed to denigrate India's effort in a field which was presumably claimed to be the sole preserve of the west. This campaign has become aggressive since India entered the West Asian markets. It is difficult to believe that some of our leaders and bureaucrats could have, wittingly or unwittingly, fallen a prey to this anti-India campaign. BHEL has already emerged as one of India's major giants capable of manufacturing a whole range of machinery and equipment for power generation. It has already established its capacity to fabricate thermal sets for the proposed super thermal power stations and to undertake maintenance, service and overhaul of sophisticated imported equipment. Indeed, the design and erection of a foundry-forge plant by BHEL's own design engineers and technical personnel is a feat which cannot be minimised. More important, BHEL has won a number of international contracts in the face of stiff competition from advanced countries and this must be regarded as a testimony of both the quality óf electrical engineering that BHEL has to offer and the competence of its engineers. BHEL's capability has already been demonstrated in the design and manufacture of hydrogenerators, a new series of AC/DC motors in IEC frames, large motors like steel-mill drives for Bokaro, 15 mw. special turbines, etc. If there was any justification for an umbrella type of agreement, perhaps the time was in the late fifties or early sixties when BHEL was struggling to set up a heavy electrical complex, not now. *(Reproduced by kind permission of The Economic Times.)*

ABBREVIATIONS AND GLOSSARY

I could have ignored the numerous acronyms and abbreviations used in India and referred instead to the various firms, laws, institutions, and concepts by their full styles, but to Indian readers that would have been misleading: BHEL is called BHEL (each letter pronounced separately), not Bharat Heavy Electricals Ltd, and the Foreign Exchange (Regulation) Act is never called anything but FERA, pronounced 'feera'. So I have put them all in—along with many others—and for good measure have included terms such as 'crore' that might not be familiar to all readers.

ADB	Asian Development Bank
ADNOC	Abu Dhabi National Oil Company
AIEI	Association of Indian Engineering Industry
BHEL	Bharat Heavy Electricals Ltd
BICC	British Insulated Callender's Cables Ltd
bn	billion (one thousand million)
BOTB	British Overseas Trade Board
cardamom	a spice
CBI	Confederation of British Industry
CES	Consulting Engineering Services Ltd
CET	Common External Tariff (of the EEC)
CMTI	Central Machine Tool Institute
COPU	Committee on Public Undertakings (of the Lok Sabha)
CPC	Chemicals and Pharmaceuticals Corporation
CPE	centrally planned economies
CP(M)	Communist Party (Marxist)
crore	ten million
DAC	Development Assistance Committee (of the OECD)
Dasturco	M. N. Dastur & Co. (P) Ltd
DCPL	Development Consultants Private Ltd
ECC	Engineering Construction Corporation
dollar	the US dollar
ECGC	Export Credit and Guarantee Corporation Ltd (of India)
ECGD	Export Credits Guarantee Department (of the UK)
ECLA	(UN) Economic Commission for Latin America
EEC	European Economic Community
EEPC	Engineering Export Promotion Council (of India)
EIL	Engineers India Ltd

EPI   Engineering Projects (India) Ltd
EPNS   Electro plated nickel silver
ESCAP   (UN) Economic and Social Commission for Asia and the
                Pacific

FAO   (UN) Food and Agriculture Organization
FCNRA   Foreign Currency (Non-Resident) Accounts
FERA   Foreign Exchange (Regulation) Act
FIEO   Federation of Indian Export Organizations
FRG   Federal Republic of Germany (West Germany)

GDP   gross domestic product
GDR   German Democratic Republic (East Germany)
GEC   The General Electric Company (of Britain)
GIL   Gammon (India) Ltd
GNP   gross national product
GOI   Government of India
GSP   Generalized Scheme of Preferences

HHEC   Handicraft and Handloom Export Corporation
HMT   Hindustan Machine Tools Ltd
HSC   Hindustan Steel Works Construction Ltd

IAAI   International Airports Authority of India
IBRD   International Bank for Reconstruction and Development
                (the World Bank)
ICDC   Industrial and Commercial Development Corporation
                (of Kenya)
ICI   Imperial Chemical Industries Ltd or Indian Chemical
                Industries Ltd (both these related firms being known as ICI)
ICICI   Industrial Credit and Investment Corporation of India Ltd
IDA   International Development Association
IDBI   Industrial Development Bank of India
IFCI   Industrial Finance Corporation of India
IIC   Indian Investment Centre
ILO   International Labour Office
IMF   International Monetary Fund
IRCC   Indian Road Construction Corporation Ltd
ISCO   International Standard Classification of Occupations
ISIC   International Standard Industrial Classification of all
                Economic Activities
ITC   Indian Tobacco Company Ltd
ITI   Indian Telephone Industries Ltd

km   kilometre
KV   kilovolt
KWU   Kraftwerk Union

LDC	less developed country
LNG	liquefied natural gas
Lok Sabha	lower house of the Indian parliament
m^3pd	cubic metres per day
MECON	Metallurgical and Engineering Consultants (India) Ltd
MFA	Multi-Fibre Arrangement (of the EEC)
MMTC	Minerals and Metals Trading Corporation of India Ltd
MRTPA	Monopolies and Restrictive Trade Practices Act
MW	megawatt
NBCC	National Buildings Construction Corporation Ltd
NIC	newly industrializing country
NIDC	National Industrial Development Corporation Ltd
NOC	No Objection Certificate
NOS	not otherwise specified
NSIC	National Small Industries Corporation
OECD	Organization for Economic Co-operation and Development
OGL	Open General Licence
OPEC	Organization of Petroleum Exporting Countries
PEC	Projects and Equipment Corporation Ltd
Rajya Sabha	upper house of the Indian parliament
R & D	Research and development
RBI	Reserve Bank of India
RITES	Rail India Technical and Economic Services Ltd
RTA	Retrospective Terms Adjustment (of aid)
SCCC	State Contracting Company for Construction (of Iraq)
SCCWASP	State Construction Company for Water and Sewerage Projects (of Iraq)
SDRs	Special Drawing Rights
SIA	Secretariat of Industrial Approvals
SITC	Standard International Trade Classification
SOB	State Organization for Buildings (of Iraq)
SOIDC	State Organization for Industrial Design and Construction (of Iraq)
SOOP	State Organization for Oil Projects (of Iraq)
SORB	State Organization for Roads and Bridges (of Iraq)
STC	State Trading Corporation of India Ltd
TCE	Tata Consulting Engineers
TCS	Tata Consultancy Services
TELCO	Tata Engineering and Locomotive Company Ltd
TISCO	Tata Iron and Steel Company Ltd
tpd (or y)	tonnes per day (or year)

UAE	United Arab Emirates
UK	United Kingdom of Great Britain and Northern Ireland
UN	United Nations
UNIDO	United Nations Industrial Development Organization
WAPCOS	Water and Power Development Consultancy Services Ltd
YAR	Yemen Arab Republic (North Yemen)
zemindar	tax farmer; later, landlord

BIBLIOGRAPHY

Abolfathi, Farid and others. *The OPEC Market to 1985*. Lexington, Mass., Lexington Books, 1977.

Association of Indian Engineering Industry. *Handbook of Statistics*. New Delhi, irregularly, every two or three years.

Balasubramanyam, V. N. *International Transfer of Technology to India*. New York, Praeger, 1973.

Bhagwati, J. N. and P. Desai. *India: Planning for Industrialization: Industrialization and Trade Policies since 1951*. London, OUP for OECD, 1970.

Bhagwati, J. N. and T. N. Srinivasan. *Foreign Trade Regimes and Economic Development*, vi: *India*. New York, National Bureau of Economic Research, 1975.

Business Standard. Calcutta, daily.

Cable, Vincent and Ann Weston. *South Asia's Exports to the EEC: Obstacles and Opportunities*. London, Overseas Development Institute, 1979.

Central Electricity Authority. *Public Electricity Supply: All-India Statistics: General Review 1976/77*. New Delhi, 1978.

Chandhok, H. L. *Wholesale Price Statistics 1947–1978*. New Delhi, Economic and Scientific Research Foundation, 1979.

Chase Manhattan Bank. *International Finance*. New York, fortnightly.

Commerce. Bombay, weekly.

Commerce Research Bureau. *Inward Remittances: Kerala: a Survey*. Bombay, Bombay Chamber of Commerce and Industry, 1978.

Confederation of British Industry. *India 1977: a Report of a British Co-operation Mission to India—November 1976—Organised Jointly by the CBI and the India, Pakistan and Bangladesh Association, and Supported by the British Overseas Trade Board*. London, CBI, 1977.

Eastern Economist. New Delhi, weekly.

Economic and Political Weekly. Bombay, weekly.

Economic Monitoring Service. *Foreign Trade Statistics of India*. Bombay, annually.

Economic Times. New Delhi, daily.

Economist. London, weekly.

Engineering Export Promotion Council. *Handbook of Export Statistics*. Calcutta, annually.

149

—— *Project Exports: Report of the Committee set up to Examine the Recommendations of the Workshop on Project Exports Organized by the Engineering Export Promotion Council at Vigyan Bhavan, New Delhi, on 28 and 29 March 1978.* Calcutta, EEPC, 1978.

Ezekiel, Hannan. *Overview.* New Delhi, Macmillan of India, 1978.

Financial Express. Bombay, daily.

Financial Times. London, daily.

Great Britain, Central Statistical Office. *Annual Abstract of Statistics.* London, HMSO.

—— Department of Trade. *Overseas Trade Statistics of the United Kingdom.* London, HMSO, annually.

—— Foreign and Commonwealth Office. *The Newly Industrialising Countries and the Adjustment Problem: Report by a Working Group.* London, HMSO 1979. (Government Economic Service Working Paper no. 18.)

—— House of Commons, Select Committee on Overseas Development. *The Pattern of UK Aid to India.* Report of 1st session of 1978/79. HC 338 (1979). London, HMSO, 1979.

—— Ministry of Overseas Development. *British Aid Statistics.* London, HMSO, annually.

—— —— *Overseas Development. The Changing Emphasis in British Aid Policies: More Help for the Poorest.* Cmnd 6270. London, HMSO, 1975.

Hindu. Madras, daily.

Hindustan Times. New Delhi, daily.

Hong Kong. *Hong Kong 1979: a Review of 1978.* Hong Kong, Government Printer, 1979.

India, Cabinet Secretariat. *Monthly Abstract of Statistics.* New Delhi, Central Statistical Organization, Department of Statistics.

—— Ministry of Commerce. *Monthly Statistics of the Foreign Trade of India.* Calcutta, Department of Commercial Intelligence and Statistics.

—— Ministry of Finance. *Economic Survey.* New Delhi, annually.

—— Ministry of Industry. *Statement on Industrial Policy.* New Delhi, 1977.

—— Ministry of Information and Broadcasting. *India 1977–78.* New Delhi, 1978.

—— Ministry of Labour. *Indian Labour Journal.* Simla, monthly.

—— Planning Commission. *Draft Five Year Plan 1978–83.* Delhi, Controller of Publications, 1978.

—— Trade Fair Authority. *Economic and Commercial News.* New Delhi, weekly.

India News. London, weekly.

Indian Engineering Exporter. Calcutta, quarterly.

Indian Express. Bombay, daily.

International Affairs. London, quarterly.

International Labour Office. *Year Book of Labour Statistics.* Geneva.

International Monetary Fund. *International Financial Statistics.* Washington, DC, monthly.

Jha, Prem Shankar. BHEL-Siemens Accord. *Economic Times,* 10 and 11 May 1979.

Kidron, Michael. *Foreign Investments in India.* London, OUP, 1965.

Kochanek, Stanley A. *Business and Politics in India.* Los Angeles, University of California Press, 1974.

Kumar, Sashi and B. Menon. 'Wealth from the Gulf: Dynamics of Change'. *Hindu* ('Weekly Magazine' section), 1 Oct. 1978.

Kumar, S. Krishna. 'Overseas Malayalees and Industrialization of Kerala'. Paper read at World Conference on Malayalam, Kerala Culture and Development, held by Kerala University at Trivandrum, 1–7 Nov. 1977.

Lal, Deepak. *Poverty, Power and Prejudice.* London, Fabian Research Series 340, 1978.

Lall, Sanjaya. Transnationals, Domestic Enterprises and Industrial Structures in Host LDCs: a Survey. *Oxford Economic Papers,* 30/2 (1978).

—— Developing Countries as Exporters of Industrial Technology. *Research Policy,* 9/1 (1980).

—— and Paul Streeten. *Foreign Investment, Transnationals and Developing Countries.* Boulder, Colo., Westview Press, 1977.

Lecraw, D. Direct Investment by Firms from Less-developed Countries. *Oxford Economic Papers,* 29/3 (1977).

Lipton, Michael and Peter Tulloch. India and the Enlarged European Community. *International Affairs* (London), 50/1 (1974).

Lipton, Michael and John Firn. *The Erosion of a Relationship: India and Britain Since 1960.* London, OUP for RIIA, 1976.

Mathew, E. T. and P. R. Gopinathan Nair. Socio-economic Characteristics of Emigrants and Emigrants' Households: a Case Study of Two Villages in Kerala. *Economic and Political Weekly,* 15 July 1978.

Middle Eastern Economic Digest. London, weekly.

Middle Eastern Economic Survey. Nicosia, weekly.

Morris, James. *Pax Britannica: the Climax of an Empire.* London, Faber & Faber, 1968.

New India Industries Ltd, Market Research Division. *Inward Remittances: Gujarat: a Survey.* Bombay, Bombay Chamber of Commerce and Industry, 1979.

New Scientist. London, weekly.

Organization for Economic Co-operation and Development. *Geographical Distribution of Financial Flows to Developing Countries*. Paris, OECD, annually.
Oxford Economic Papers. Oxford, quarterly.

Pachauri, R. K. *Energy and Economic Development in India*. New York, Praeger, 1977.
Prakash, B. A. Impact of Foreign Remittances: a Case Study of Chavakkad Village in Kerala. *Economic and Political Weekly*, 8 July 1978.

Research Policy. Amsterdam, quarterly.
Reserve Bank of India. *Annual Report*. Bombay.
—— *Reserve Bank of India Bulletin*. Bombay, monthly.

Singh, Manmohan. *India's Export Trends*. Oxford, Clarendon Press, 1964.
Singh, Tarlok. *India's Development Experience*. London, Macmillan, 1974.
Statesman. Calcutta, daily.

Tata Services Ltd. *Statistical Outline of India*. Bombay, TSL, Dept of Economics and Statistics, annually.
Times. London, daily.
Times of India. New Delhi, daily.

United Nations. *Monthly Bulletin of Statistics*. New York, UN.
—— *Statistical Yearbook*. New York, UN.

Veit, Lawrence A. *India's Second Revolution: the Dimensions of Development*. New York, McGraw-Hill for Council on Foreign Relations [1976].

INDEX

Abu Dhabi
  construction projects, 24, 35 n.8, 75,
    139
  see also United Arab Emirates
Afghanistan
  power and irrigation project, 31
Aid to India from
  Canada, 86, 128
  Czechoslovakia, 27
  Japan, 128
  main donors, 128
  Soviet Union, 4, 27
  UK, 4, 86–9, 100, 128, 129–30
    tied to purchase of British goods
    and services, 85, 87–9
  USA, 4, 27, 86, 128
  West Germany, 4, 128
Algeria: projects
  petrochemicals, 31
  plant and machinery, 27, 31
Asia Foundations & Constructions Pvt
  Ltd
  Iraq: bridge construction, 132
  oil jetty fender piles, 132
Association of Indian Engineering
  Industry, 7, 38–9, 101
Auto & General Manufacturing Co.
  Kuwait: plant and machinery, 134

Bahrain
  Indian labour force, 49; remittances,
    53
Balmer Lawrie & Co., 24
  Kuwait: electrical repair workshop,
    joint venture, 135
  UAE: container plant, joint venture,
    140
  oil lubricants plant, contract, 139
Bangladesh
  iron and steel plants, feasibility
    studies, 31
B.G. Shirke, 23
  Saudi Arabia: design consultancy for
    buildings, 138
  UAE: house building, 139

Bharat Heavy Electricals Ltd, 17, 27–9,
  79, 87
  collaboration with
    British firms, 69, 102
    West German firms, 27, 69–70, 92,
      142–3
  consultancy services, 18, 30
  projects in
    Libya: extension of Tripoli West
      power station, 24, 28, 74–5, 136
    Malaysia: boilers and telecom-
      munications, 27–9, 31–2
    New Zealand: hydro generators, 29
    Saudi Arabia: electrification pro-
      ject at Wadi Jizan, xi–xii, 28,
      36 n.13, 66, 73, 94, 138
Bhutan: power and irrigation, 31
Birla Consultancy Pvt Ltd, 30
  Sudan: textile mills, feasibility studies,
    33
Birla Group, 23, 66, 92–3
Blue Star Engineering
  Kuwait: water coolers, joint venture,
    135
Bombay Suburban Electric Supply Ltd
  Saudi Arabia: electrification project
    at Wadi Jizan, sub-contract, xii,
    138
Borneo
  Indian migrant labour, 51
Braithwaite & Co.
  Kuwait: pressed steel tanks, 134
Bridge & Roof Co. (India) Ltd, 24
  Iraq: sewerage schemes, 25, 132
  Syria: cement plant, technical ser-
    vices, 33
British Aerospace, 101
British Insulated Callender's Cables,
  94, 102, 103
British Overseas Trade Board, 101
Burma
  Indian migrant labour, 51
  power and irrigation, 31
Burmah Oil, 91

153